"A gem of a resource for anyone who struggles with anxiety or worry. Reinecke makes the difficulties of anxiety so much easier to understand with his gentle and encouraging guidance. He pinpoints the typical thoughts and reactions that anxiety triggers, then offers effective questions to ask yourself and healing activities to apply right away. This great little book gets right to the point with inspiring quotes, no-nonsense information, gentle understanding, and superb recommendations."

—Denise D. Davis, Ph.D., clinical psychologist and assistant director of clinical training at Vanderbilt University in Nashville, TN

"Anxiety is inevitable; we need it to survive. Sometimes, however, we are stuck in it. This book is a place where evidence-based science meets philosophy of life. Everybody should have it: those who are struggling with anxiety, those who are helping people to overcome anxiety, and those who like to think about human nature. Once read, give this book a stable place in your library. If it happens that old worries come to mind again, it means only that some of the lessons from this book may be worth coming back to."

—Agnieszka Popiel, MD, Ph.D., psychiatrist and cognitive behavioral therapist at Warsaw School of Science and Humanities and president of the Polish Association for Behavioural and Cognitive Therapists

"Problematic anxiety is common and presents itself in diverse ways. Mark Reinecke skillfully takes what is shared amongst various anxiety concerns and concisely presents a great deal of information. He asks questions that will make the reader reevaluate and offers sensible strategies that are based upon research evidence. If anxiety is impairing the life you want to live, you will most certainly find useful information in this book."

—Maureen L. Whittal, Ph.D., ABPP, associate professor at the University of British Columbia in Vancouver, BC

"Reinecke's *Little Ways to Keep Calm and Carry On* immediately engages and informs readers as both a how-to handbook and valuable reference. His twenty priceless lessons can help anyone work through worries and become happier with results that last. This little gem should be on everyone's self-improvement shelf."

—Paul L. Corona, Ph.D., director of learning and organization development at Northwestern University in Evanston, IL

"Little Ways to Keep Calm and Carry On will have a big impact. Reinecke effectively translates the complex theories behind evidence-based anxiety treatment into usable and user-friendly practical actions. His book presents readers with a clear understanding of how anxiety can wreak havoc on their lives and guides them through a step-by-step process that will free them of this distress. His solution-focused and optimistic approach is a welcome addition to the field."

—Golda S. Ginsburg, Ph.D., associate professor of psychiatry at the Johns Hopkins University School of Medicine in Baltimore, MD

"This accessible book describes some of the most common and effective techniques used by cognitive behavioral therapists in the treatment of anxiety and stress. The volume is unique in its direct, no-nonsense style, and will help readers identify and deal with unhelpful thoughts, behaviors, and symptoms. A handy guide for finding a personal combination of techniques that will help you carry on."

—Adrian Wells, Ph.D., consultant clinical psychologist and professor of clinical and experimental psychopathology at the University of Manchester, UK

"Reineke's book provides a compact and succinct overview of how to identify and deal with the everyday forms of stress and anxiety that many people encounter in their lives. If you are looking to find new ways to cope, this book will help you to do so."

—Cheryl Carmin, Ph.D., professor at the University of Illinois at Chicago and director of its stress and anxiety disorders clinic and cognitive behavior therapy program

LITTLE WAYS TO

KEEP
CALM
AND
CARRY
ON

• •

TWENTY LESSONS FOR MANAGING
WORRY, ANXIETY, AND FEAR

MARK A. REINECKE, PH.D.

New Harbinger Publications, Inc.

Publisher's Note

This publication is designed to provide accurate and authoritative information in regard to the subject matter covered. It is sold with the understanding that the publisher is not engaged in rendering psychological, financial, legal, or other professional services. If expert assistance or counseling is needed, the services of a competent professional should be sought.

Distributed in Canada by Raincoast Books

Copyright © 2010 by Mark Reinecke
New Harbinger Publications, Inc.
5674 Shattuck Avenue
Oakland, CA 94609
www.newharbinger.com

Cover design by Amy Shoup; Text design by Michele Waters-Kermes; Acquired by Melissa Kirk; Edited by Nelda Street

---

Library of Congress Cataloging-in-Publication Data

Reinecke, Mark A.
  Little ways to keep calm and carry on : twenty lessons for managing worry, anxiety, and fear / Mark A. Reinecke.
      p. cm.
  Includes bibliographical references.
  ISBN 978-1-57224-881-6
  1. Anxiety. 2. Worry. 3. Fear. 4. Self-help techniques. I. Title.
  BF575.A6R36 2010
  152.4'6--dc22

                    2010020131

12   11   10

10   9   8   7   6   5   4   3   2   1   First printing

Mixed Sources
Product group from well-managed forests, controlled sources and recycled wood or fiber
www.fsc.org Cert no. SW-COC-000952
© 1996 Forest Stewardship Council

This book is printed with soy ink.

To my wife Marsha and my daughter Gracie, with love.

To Aaron Beck and Arthur Freeman, with greatest appreciation.

CONTENTS

	Acknowledgments	**VII**
	About the title	**IX**
	Introduction	**1**
LESSON 1	Anxiety: It Works	**5**
LESSON 2	The Big "A"	**10**
LESSON 3	We Overestimate Risk When We're Afraid	**15**
LESSON 4	The Future Is Uncertain	**19**
LESSON 5	Influence and Control	**24**
LESSON 6	You Have the Power to Control Your Level of Anxiety	**29**
LESSON 7	Perfect Solutions Don't Exist	**36**

LESSON 8   Sometimes You Can Take Control of Bad Situations—but Sometimes Not   41

LESSON 9   Recurring, Intrusive Thoughts Are Normal; It's the Meaning We Attach to Them That Counts   46

LESSON 10   Dwelling on Problems Impairs Your Ability to Cope   51

LESSON 11   Worrying Is Highly Overrated   56

LESSON 12   Don't Magnify the Importance of Your Physical Sensations   61

LESSON 13   It's Time to Relax   66

LESSON 14   Evaluate Your Thoughts and Make Them Account for Themselves   73

LESSON 15   Changing Your Thoughts   81

LESSON 16   When You're Worried or Anxious, Avoiding Problems Is Among the Worst Things You Can Do   89

LESSON 17   Social Anxiety: Worrying Too Much About What Others Think   96

LESSON 18   What's Really on Your Mind?   103

LESSON 19   Flow with the Current of Life   110

LESSON 20   Live Wisely   114

Epilogue: A Final Note   119

Resources for Readers   121

References   123

ACKNOWLEDGMENTS

Having had the opportunity to know and work with a large number of clinical scholars over the past twenty years, I have the honor of counting them as not only colleagues but also friends. Their research has formed and clarified our understanding of anxiety and supported the development of ever more effective treatment strategies. Because their work is the foundation on which this book is built, they are, in a sense, coexplorers and coauthors in this endeavor. It is my pleasure to acknowledge the following professionals' important contributions to my understanding of anxiety and to the work described in this book: Judy Beck, Tom Borkovec, Gillian Butler, John Cacioppo, John Calamari, Cheryl Carmin, David Clark, Frank Dattilio, Edna Foa, Marty Franklin, Jackie Gollan, Rick Heimberg, Stefan Hofmann, Deb Hope, Robert Leahy, Rich McNally, Doug Mennin, Sue Mineka, Costas Papageorgiou, Ronald Rapee, Paul Salkovskis, Gail Steketee,

John Teasdale, Adrian Wells, Jesse Wright, and Rick Zinbarg. Finally, I would like to offer my sincere thanks to my editors Jess Beebe and Melissa Kirk and to the rest of the staff at New Harbinger. Their expert guidance and astute recommendations have been indispensable in bringing this book to life.

# ABOUT THE TITLE

Nineteen thirty-nine was a dark and savage year in Europe. Hitler and the Nazi army had annexed Austria and Czechoslovakia, and on September 1, Hitler launched his Blitzkrieg attack on Poland. Two days later, France and Great Britain declared war on Germany. World War II had begun. The title of this book and the small crown, are based upon a motivational poster published by the British government that same year. Long forgotten, a copy of the poster was found in a used bookstore in Northumberland, England in 2000. The poster has since become a popular, even iconic, message of resilience in the face of adversity. Simple. reassuring, and inspiring, it remains an encouraging sentiment in difficult time.

INTRODUCTION

Worrying is a national epidemic, so if you feel anxious and uncertain, you're not alone. But there's good news! Thanks to researchers and clinicians, this subject is well understood. Here it is: a quick, compact read that tells you what you need to know to understand anxiety and deal with it constructively. This little book presents the most important findings from empirical research in cognitive behavioral therapy and affective neuroscience in a concise way that's easy to grasp. It tells you what you need to know and do. Based on recent work in empirically supported anxiety treatments, this easy-to-read guide will help you deal with an emotion that can completely unravel your day.

Think of this book as a tool that teaches you how to filter your thoughts in ways that will change both how you feel and how you behave. Despite the simplicity of the techniques, they produce powerful results.

Read each lesson in sequence. Some will resonate with you more than others, but each lesson allows you to build your own customized "anxiety management toolbox."

As you read this book, consider taking some time to write your thoughts. Put pen to paper and note how you might apply the various lessons in your life. This is your own personal journey—an opportunity to learn to think, feel, and behave differently. You might think of your notes as a personal journal or a private blog. Keeping a journal is entirely optional, but writing notes and reflecting on new information will not only aid your retention but also help you organize the material in your mind and integrate it with your existing knowledge. It may make for a richer and more useful experience, and it should only take a few minutes. Give it a try.

Many of the lessons conclude with recommendations for action, under the headings "Now Ask Yourself..." and "What You Need to Do." For these activities, you'll need a notebook or at least a few blank sheets of paper. Though brief, these exercises can be quite powerful. Applying daily what you've learned can accelerate the process, increasing your likelihood of making progress and maintaining your gains. These are the tools that will help you master your worry, anxiety, and fear. Clinicians often refer to them as "homework," but this isn't homework in the academic sense. Rather, it's the notion that though insight alone—what we learn—may not bring about changes in emotions or behavior, we can introduce change by acting on our knowledge and insight. You'll want to apply this insight in your day-to-day life, and these exercises are an opportunity to do just that.

Know this: these approaches work. I've seen them work with my clients. More importantly, dozens of controlled studies completed at clinics and research centers around the world support the approaches described in this book. The result? Using them can help you have a better day—one where you are more productive, have a greater sense of control, and manage whatever life throws your way by using solutions rather than letting worry take your brain hostage. A small book is no substitute for professional care, of course. If you are experiencing more severe anxiety, or thoughts of death or suicide, you'll want to work with an experienced mental health specialist; you'll find Internet resources at the end of the book.

Don't underestimate the power of worry, anxiety, and fear. When appropriate, they can play a positive, even essential, role in your life. However, they can also be disruptive and disabling. The bottom line is that you don't have to be a victim of these unpleasant emotions. You can control how you live your day and what role anxiety plays, and this little guide will show you how.

Let's get on with it.

LESSON 1

ANXIETY: IT WORKS

Courage is resistance to fear, mastery of fear—
not absence of fear.

—Mark Twain

Based in the oldest areas of the brain, anxiety is *highly* adaptive. It alerts us to potential dangers in our environment and impels us to take action. Anxiety and fear are essential for our survival (Cosmides and Tooby 2000). All people experience anxiety, and this has been true since the beginning of time; that's how the human brain is wired.

Back in the sixties, there was a popular television show called *Lost in Space*. One of the main characters was a robot that would light up and exclaim, "Danger, danger, danger!" on a fairly regular basis. This was a signal warning all the characters to be alert. Your own brain operates very much like this robot. Anxiety is your brain's way of alerting you to a potential threat or danger in your environment, and like the robot in the show, it's very difficult to ignore.

When your brain perceives a threat, it assesses the environment for responses to two quick questions: *How big of a threat is it?* and *Can I manage it or avoid it?* The level of anxiety you feel matches how significant you perceive the threat or danger to be, as well as how confident you are in your ability to cope (Freeman et al. 1990). Let's look at an example.

A Neanderthal man is sitting in his cave when a snarling bear appears at the entrance. The man perceives the danger and becomes (quite reasonably) anxious. His brain all but instantly perceives the threat and evaluates the danger (high risk). He realizes he can't escape and is defenseless (low coping), so his level of fear soars.

Now, let's take the same scenario but change the man's perceptions. The same snarling bear enters the cave (high risk), but the man has a club. Seeing that the bear is in a tight entrance, where it can't stand upright or maneuver, the man thinks, "I've got the advantage [high coping]. I'm ready, and I'm going after him. I'll have some food and a fur blanket for winter [moderate anxiety, adaptive coping]."

Now, let's look at a more contemporary scenario. Your boss calls you into his office and says, "The bottom line's really bad. I'm sorry, but we're going to have to let you go in thirty days." Your brain (quite reasonably) perceives the threat. You begin to think, *No paycheck! I won't be able to pay the bills or my mortgage, and I'll lose my house! I don't know what I can do!* And your anxiety soars.

Now, let's change the perceptions. Your boss calls you into his office and says, "Your job is over in thirty days." But this time, you think, *I haven't been happy in this job for a long, long time, and this company is on a downward slope. Now is as good a time as any for a change.* You continue by noting, *I've got a good skill set, and I've always wanted to start a company of my own. Perhaps this is the push I need to make a change. This could be a great opportunity. I don't like it, but I can handle it* (high coping, moderate anxiety).

The stimulus in each of the previous examples is exactly the same, but the emotional responses are entirely different. In the first scenario, the worry machine is turned on full force. In the second one, the anxiety is lower because of the positive perception of the ability to cope.

KEY POINTS

- Anxiety is adaptive. It signals a perceived threat.

- How anxious you become depends on two things:

  1. How significant you perceive the threat to be

  2. Your perceived ability to cope—that is, how well you think you can manage this threat

- You control these two perceptions. If you change them, you can feel less anxious.

WHAT YOU MAY BE THINKING

My mind doesn't come equipped with a volume control that I can turn up or down to control the level of anxiety I feel. It isn't that simple. Besides, the things I'm worried about are real. I'm not exaggerating; these things could happen. I feel very afraid and uncertain. I just want these feelings to go away.

NOW ASK YOURSELF...

- Are there situations where you tend to exaggerate the risk of negative outcomes? Do you "awfulize" or magnify how bad it will be?

- Are there situations where you tend to underestimate your ability to manage problems? How often does this happen?

- Think about three or four recent events in your life that caused you to feel anxious or worried. Did you anticipate negative outcomes that never happened? Did you make it harder on yourself by anticipating the worst-case scenario? How did this make you feel?

WHAT YOU NEED TO DO

1. Rather than exaggerate or magnify how awful things will be, strive to accurately assess risky situations.

2. Start by making a list of the two or three situations or problems that generate the most stress or anxiety in your life. What thoughts flow through your mind at these times? How strongly do you believe them?

3. Once you have your list, we'll look at how you think about these situations, how you feel, and how you respond. But first, let's discuss how anxiety, an essential part of a complex emotional system, works. This is covered in lesson 2.

LESSON 2

THE BIG "A"

Oh the nerves, the nerves—the mysteries of this machine called man! Oh the little that unhinges it, poor creatures that we are!

—Alderman Cute, in "The Chimes," by Charles Dickens

Simply said, anxiety is an emotion—but what an emotion it is! Anxiety, like all emotions, has three components: biological (your physical response), cognitive (your accompanying perceptions and thoughts), and behavioral (your actions) (Frijda 1986).

When you experience a high level of anxiety, all other emotions are subservient to the big "A." This is for a reason. Anxiety not only alerts you to a potential danger but also prepares you for action: signals are sent to the adrenal glands to release adrenalin, increasing your heart rate and converting glycogen to glucose for energy; your facial expressions change, alerting others; your muscles tense and your respiration rate increases, preparing you to fight or flee; your pupils dilate, bringing in more visual information; and you begin to retrieve memories of similar situations from the past, allowing you to select the best course of action. Anxiety organizes your priorities (it's *very* hard to think about anything but your safety when a bear is staring at you) and motivates you into goal-directed action (to address the risk). Just as importantly, anxiety carries meaning. We reflect on events that lead us to become anxious, fearful, or worried. We strive to make sense of them, to understand how they are related to other life experiences, and to determine what they portend for the future. We don't simply respond to stressful or frightening life events, we ascribe meaning to them. So anxiety is part of a complex, intricately calibrated biological and cognitive system that has evolved over aeons to facilitate our survival by protecting us from danger.

Quite simply, your body braces for action when the big "A" takes its cue. In a matter of seconds, your body reacts biologically, cognitively, and behaviorally—all in response to a perceived threat. The key word here is "perceived." As a warning system, anxiety alerts us that something *may* be wrong, not that something *is* wrong. When nature's alarm bell sounds, we need to listen, reflect on it, and determine whether there's actually a danger or it's a false alarm.

As we've seen, although it is often uncomfortable to experience, anxiety is a natural and useful state. It's a particularly good thing if you happen to be faced with life-threatening danger. It helps you quickly organize your priorities, focus your attention, and prepare to respond. You give whatever you are afraid of immediate attention, which prepares you to react rapidly and flexibly. It's an amazing system!

But difficulties can arise when the big "A" is activated several times a day. This is when anxiety can wreak havoc. When we allow ourselves to perceive small annoyances as big threats, anxiety is no longer useful. Continuous, high levels of arousal can bring on tension headaches, stomach ailments, fatigue, and a host of other physical symptoms. Just as importantly, chronic anxiety or worry tends to push away all the other priorities in your life. Ever had days when all you did was push papers around? Chances are your brain was pulled toward an anxiety-triggered priority, not allowing you to focus on anything else. We all know those days; often they result in a high level of frustration, because we can't get even simple tasks done. But there's good news. You have quite a bit of control over when you allow the big "A" to take hold. With practice, you can modulate your emotions and constructively direct your anxiety.

KEY POINTS

- Anxiety is part of a biologically based system. Because physiological, cognitive, and behavioral changes are also in play, anxiety is more than just a feeling.

- To successfully manage anxiety, you need to address all three parts of the system.

- Some anxiety is good, but continual anxiety can wear down the body, both physically and mentally, potentially leading to indecisiveness, depression, and serious illness.

WHAT YOU MAY BE THINKING

This makes sense, but if it's biological, doesn't that mean I need medication? These thoughts and worries I've been having almost have a life of their own. I wonder if I'm just wired to worry. Some days, I feel paralyzed by all of this. I'm not sure anything will work.

NOW ASK YOURSELF...

1. How many times a day does the big "A" surface?

2. What are your physical symptoms when you feel anxious or worried?

3. How do these feelings affect your behavior? Do your anxious thoughts interfere with your ability to accomplish things in the moment?

WHAT YOU NEED TO DO

- Be aware of how you respond to the big "A." Begin to monitor it. What are the most common triggers? What physical symptoms do you experience? How does it affect your behavior?

- Lesson 3 will help you put the brakes on worry.

LESSON 3

WE OVERESTIMATE RISK WHEN WE'RE AFRAID

There is nothing either good or bad but thinking makes it so.

—Hamlet, in *Hamlet* (act 2, scene2),
by William Shakespeare

The most important things to do when you feel anxious about a situation are get accurate facts and make an accurate assessment. When something bad happens, we tend to overestimate the likelihood that it will happen again (Matthews and MacLeod 1994).

After 9/11, a large majority of Americans surveyed believed another terrorist attack was forthcoming. They believed a terrorist would harm them or someone they knew within one year. Because the 9/11 attacks were a horrific experience for all Americans, it was perfectly normal for people to feel this way.

However, the number of attacks in the United States during the year following 9/11 was zero. So the lesson here is about keeping things in perspective. Fear tends to distort our assessments, at least for the short term.

It's important to have a conversation with yourself when something bad happens or when you perceive a threat. When you become anxious, ask yourself the following questions:

1. What exactly do you fear will happen?

2. What's the likelihood that this feared event will occur?

3. What's the most likely scenario?

4. Are there protective factors (what psychologists refer to as "safety cues") that suggest the feared event might not occur or might not be so bad if it does happen?

5. How will you cope with or manage the most likely scenario? Try to quantify it. Be as specific as possible in detailing what the most likely scenario will be.

KEY POINTS

- Size up the situation by gathering accurate facts and making an accurate assessment.

- Identify exactly what you fear will occur, and determine the likelihood that it will happen.

- Don't overestimate; base your decisions (and emotions) on accurate, valid numbers and assessments of risk.

WHAT YOU MAY BE THINKING

How can I be sure my assessment is correct? What if I've left something out or I haven't properly evaluated every possible scenario? What if I make a mistake?

NOW ASK YOURSELF...

1. What's the one problem in your life that you worry about the most? For this problem, what outcome do you fear the most?

2. Realistically, what's the probability that this event will happen?

3. Is there any reason to think that this event may not happen? Are there safety cues?

4. Based on all the facts you have, what's the most likely outcome?

5. What coping skills do you have to manage this outcome?

WHAT YOU NEED TO DO

- Relax and step through the problem logically. Perhaps you have a trusted friend who can help you size up the most likely scenario.

- On a notepad, list the most probable outcomes, using as much accurate information and detail as possible. Next, make a list of what you fear the most, and cross off what's not realistic. As far as waiting to see if your fears come to pass, the hard part is managing uncertainty, which is covered in the next lesson.

LESSON 4

THE FUTURE IS UNCERTAIN

Each of us needs to withdraw from the cares
which will not withdraw from us.

—Maya Angelou
(*Wouldn't Take Nothing for My Journey Now*, 1993)

This is perhaps the hardest lesson of all. We all want to feel secure and know that our future and our loved ones' futures will turn out all right. When confronted with danger or the unknown, we seek security; we want a guarantee. Herein lies the problem, because the future is unknowable. However much we would like a guarantee, we can't have it. The future is unknown. So we all need to expand our tolerance for ambiguity and uncertainty (Dugas, Gosselin, and Ladouceur 2001). We need to relinquish our desire for a guarantee.

Everyone gets a share of heartache, loss, and disappointment. At times, life can be sad, hard, and downright unfair. As Thomas Hobbes stated in 1651, the natural life of man is "solitary, poor, nasty, brutish, and short." To be sure, this is not entirely true. There is, however, always that *possibility* that worse things will occur. It's when we dwell on those extreme, unlikely possibilities that our sense of inner security begins to dissolve.

Just because things are going well doesn't mean you are secure. On the other hand, you won't necessarily feel insecure every time things aren't going well. Security comes from within you, not from what happens in your life from one day to the next. Although there are virtually no guarantees in life, you do have a certain amount of personal control or influence.

Although life is unpredictable, you are the master of the decisions you make and how you perceive events. In that sense, you are at the controls of this ride through life. Security comes from accepting ambiguity and recognizing that you can manage whatever life throws your way! As you move through the lessons in this book, you will learn how feeling secure stems from a sense of personal efficacy, or influence, confidence, and optimism.

KEY POINTS

- The future is unknowable; there are no guarantees.

- Feeling secure (and less anxious) requires us to accept ambiguity and our inability to predict the future.

- True security comes from within, not from without; it comes from perceiving ourselves as having personal "efficacy" or a sense of confidence in our ability to manage important events in our lives.

- When you feel anxious or worried, it's essential to recognize that you can control how you steer your thoughts and perceptions; you are always the one in the driver's seat of your life.

WHAT YOU MAY BE THINKING

I really don't like this part. This is what keeps me awake at night. Just because you tell me to feel secure won't make me feel that way. Yes, I want control or, at least, to feel that I have control. You just told me I have to accept the unknown, so how can I feel in control when I don't know what's going to happen?

NOW ASK YOURSELF...

- *We can't control or predict the future.* How do you feel about this statement?

- Who is the most secure person you know? Why do you think that person feels secure?

- What's the downside of accepting that you can't predict or control events? What are the benefits of adopting this perspective?

WHAT YOU NEED TO DO

1. This is, indeed, the hardest lesson of all. Realize that everyone, even the most secure person, has to accept the unknown. We can't control or predict the future.

2. The alternative is to maintain a sense of optimism and to influence events to the best of our ability. Expending a lot of energy anticipating negative outcomes only eats away at our sense of control and hope. Accepting the unpredictability of life and letting go of the need for control is actually a healthy, sensible way to approach the unknown.

3. How can we let go in this way? Adopting a mindful stance—focusing on our experience in the present moment, rather than on the future or past—can help.

4. Alternatively, you can adopt a rational stance: logically, we see that we have limited control over future events. Although we can't control the future, we can control how we respond to it. With this in mind, consciously model your behavior after someone who approaches adversity with confidence, faith, compassion, and a sense of humor.

5. Finally, reflect on situations in your past when an unexpected event challenged you. How would you characterize your response to situations you handled well? How about situations where you felt overwhelmed? In comparing your reactions to these events, what do you see? Flexibility, composure, and optimism are often more adaptive— that is, they allow us to handle challenges better—than the need for control and a guarantee that things will work out.

LESSON 5

INFLUENCE AND CONTROL

That the birds of worry and care fly over your head,
this you cannot change; but that they build
nests in your hair, this you can prevent.

—Chinese proverb

Though we'd like to have complete control over what happens in our lives, we know that's not realistic. Most things that happen in our lives are multiply determined; that is, a whole range of factors often influences them. Sometimes problems evolve over time. Moreover, the things we tend to worry about the most—health, financial security, relationships, events at work or the office—are usually complex. However much we would like to control them, to make them turn out as we wish, we simply can't.

Nevertheless, it's worth keeping in mind that we can *influence* events in our lives. So we might think of control as existing on a continuum from 0 percent (no control whatsoever) to 100 percent (complete control). Between these end points are degrees of influence ranging from just a bit to quite a lot. Although we can't control events, we can often influence them. So when you're confronting a stressful or anxiety-laden situation, it can help to ask, "How might I be able to influence this? How can I guide the outcome?"

Interestingly, it's our *perception* of our ability to influence a situation that determines the level of anxiety we feel. In a remarkable study completed in 1989 by William Sanderson, Ronald Rapee, and David Barlow, people who experienced panic attacks (severe and unexpected surges of anxiety) were asked to self-induce panic attacks by inhaling a gas that would be administered through masks they wore. They were told they could control the level of the gas by turning a knob whenever a light was illuminated on a control panel at their desks. For half of the participants, the light turned on and they could adjust the gas; not surprisingly, they experienced few panic attacks. For the others, the light didn't turn on, the gas flowed, and they were battered by panic attacks. Moreover, they rated their symptoms as more intense, experienced higher levels of anxiety, and reported a greater number of catastrophic thoughts. Being able to control the gas allowed participants to control the panic, right? Here's the trick: both groups of participants received the same high level of gas. Moreover, the knobs did nothing. They didn't regulate the flow of gas. The only real difference between the groups was whether the light came on. The difference between the people who experienced surging anxiety and those who didn't was their *perception* of control—that is, the belief that they could influence the situation.

How is this important in day-to-day life? When you're confronted by stressful, even threatening, events, it's important to keep in mind that, very often, we can influence the outcome. Moreover, it's critically important that we not lose sight of our influence. When we perceive ourselves as helpless (important outcomes are out of our control), we're more likely to become anxious.

WHAT YOU MAY BE THINKING

I should perceive I have control, perceive I can influence things—so far, so good. I'm confused, though. The folks in the study didn't really have control. The knob didn't do anything. Isn't this just trickery? It seems inauthentic—make yourself think you have control over events in your life, even if you don't.

NOW ASK YOURSELF...

- Have there been situations where you felt things were out of your control, that there was nothing you could do? How did this lead you to feel? How did this lead you to respond?

- Were there situations where you felt helpless but weren't? Were there things you could have done to manage a situation that you didn't see at the time?

- When you recognize that you can influence events and control how you think about them, how do you feel?

WHAT YOU NEED TO DO

1. Describe the problem or situation that troubles you the most. What are the various factors (or people) that are influencing this situation? How much influence does each of them have in this situation?

2. On a piece of paper, draw a continuum from 0 to 100 percent. Place a mark on the line delineating the percentage of influence you have. It's

probably not zero. You have some influence over the outcome. Are there ways of influencing the situation that you may have overlooked? Might you have more influence than you perceive? How can we move the mark higher on the continuum of control?

3. Is there any way for you to increase your influence? Might you have additional opportunities to influence the situation? If the answer is yes, how can you put them into action? What do you need to do? If the answer is no, you'll want to fully exploit what influence you do have. Again, what do you need to do? Beyond this, you'll want to acknowledge that there are other influences in play. However much we'd like to, we often can't control the future.

LESSON 6

YOU HAVE THE POWER TO CONTROL YOUR LEVEL OF ANXIETY

Remember that you are an actor in a play, and the playwright chooses the manner of it.

—Epictetus

Here's a bit of review from lesson 1: the level of anxiety we feel is basically determined by our perception of threat and our perceived ability to manage that threat. Let's put this into an equation:

Anxiety $= f$ (impending threat) (impaired coping)

Let's look at the second term in this equation, which is the perception of impending threat. Again, you decide how you are going to perceive the threat.

There are two things we consider when we assign a level of anxiety to a threatening event: the likelihood that the terrible event will happen and our estimation of how awful it will be. Just as we tend to overestimate likelihood, we also often overestimate the awfulness: we "catastrophize" (Beck 1976). Put simply, we tend to focus our attention on the worst-case scenario. Why do we do that?

We all have an occasional "tabloid" mentality when dealing with events in our lives. Just like a tabloid newspaper at the checkout line that demands your attention with huge, bold headlines, we shout this perceived awfulness to ourselves and magnify the negativity of the situation. Why? As we've seen, anxiety focuses our attention (it's hard to focus on your plans for the evening when you think you're about to get hit by a bus), motivates action (you really *should* jump out of the way), and activates memories of similar situations in our past so we can recall strategies that might work. Attention, motivation, and improved memory are all good things. The problem, of course, is that the worst-case scenario rarely occurs. We do ourselves a disservice when we "awfulize" life events and perceive things as worse than they really are. It ramps up our anxiety level to a point where it impairs our ability to handle the problem.

Awfulizing events has another consequence: it makes it difficult for us to let go of problems. As we've seen, anxiety leads us to scan the environment, searching for signs of risk. We become hypervigilant, searching and searching for signs of danger. Like a supersensitive radar system, we scan our world, looking for signs of risk. When one appears, we quickly lock onto it. At the same time, we experience difficulty letting go of focusing on these cues once the danger has passed. We stay locked on. Psychologists refer to this process as disengagement from the stimuli, and it normally occurs *very* quickly (in hundredths of a second) after a person experiences an anxiety-provoking event. Anxious people, however, often have difficulty disengaging from frightening events, cues, or stimuli. When managing our anxiety, an important strategy is learning to let go, to disengage our attention from the frightening event.

So it's important to evaluate situations with the least amount of emotion possible. Don't magnify, awfulize, or exaggerate. Rather, think of the *most likely* scenario. Think realistically about the threat and do a reality check on how the event will most likely play out. As the philosopher and psychologist William James remarked, "The art of being wise is the art of knowing what to overlook." If the truly awful event isn't likely to occur, don't spend time worrying about it. At the same time, let go of your attention to the event and disengage from it once the risk has passed.

KEY POINTS

- When something bad happens or you perceive a threat, how terrible you assess the potential outcome to be filters your reaction.

- Quite often we jump to the worst-case scenario.

- Although thinking about these potentially disastrous scenarios can serve a useful function, it comes at a cost: it unnecessarily magnifies our feelings of worry and anxiety. Once again, you control this process. You control how you perceive the threat.

- However useful it is to be aware of dangers and risks in your world, it's also helpful to disengage from them when the risk has passed.

WHAT YOU MAY BE THINKING

Are you telling me that I can control these headlines in my brain? I've always believed that you plan for the worst and hope for the best! Doesn't a lot of worrying really equal better planning?

NOW ASK YOURSELF...

1. Many people feel it's helpful, even essential, to prepare for the worst-case scenario. What do you think? From your experience, do better solutions come from planning for the worst? Are there limits or shortcomings to adopting this approach?

2. Can you think of a situation where planning for the worst-case scenario was helpful? Can you think of one where it truly paid dividends? How about the opposite? Can you think of situations where ruminating about the worst-case scenario didn't help you cope?

3. All told, do you wish you had spent more or less time ruminating about the worst-case scenario?

WHAT YOU NEED TO DO

1. Realize that focusing on the worst-case scenario often makes the problem worse.

2. In most cases, planning for the worst doesn't make for a better outcome. Rather, it leads to rumination and unnecessary worry. With this in mind, what are the two or three most likely outcomes for the problem you are facing?

3. There are two components to disengagement: determining that the danger has passed and redirecting your attention. With this in mind, what evidence do you have that the problem you've identified might ultimately be resolved? That it has an end point? That the danger has passed or may be lessening?

4. Now, make a list of four or five activities that would be truly engrossing for you, activities that would fully absorb your attention. They may be enjoyable activities (such as reading, knitting, playing a sport, completing a crossword, or working as a volunteer) or a challenging "mastery" activity (developing a new skill that requires focus and persistence). Try them out. Disengage from the fearful thought or event.

5. A technical point is in order here: before you disengage or distract, be completely sure you perceive that the risk has passed. You'll know this if your feelings of anxiety are lower and you're feeling relatively calm. Now you disengage from the thought or situation. Don't disengage or turn away at the height of your anxiety. This will simply serve as evidence that the danger is real and that you can't handle it—magnifying the anxiety. Rather, stay with the anxiety-provoking situation, demonstrate to yourself that it's manageable, and then put it aside: disengage.

6. Psychologists refer to this process of staying with an anxiety-provoking event until the anxiety subsides as *habituation*, and it's among the most powerful tools for overcoming anxiety. *Systematic desensitization* (Wolpe 1982) builds on this principle. By systematically approaching a series of ever more challenging events, allowing yourself to feel the anxiety, and allowing the anxiety to resolve or habituate without turning away or avoiding, you can develop a sense of confidence and mastery. You'll find that you're now coping with the thing you'd feared! Give it a try!

LESSON 7

PERFECT SOLUTIONS DON'T EXIST

Success is the ability to go from one failure to another with no loss of enthusiasm.

—Winston Churchill

When we become anxious, we often misread events by magnifying how bad things are, exaggerating the risk involved, overlooking evidence of security (what researchers refer to as "safety cues"), and selectively attending to danger signs. These perceptual biases and cognitive distortions can amplify our anxiety (Beck, Emery, and Greenberg 1985). Among the most disabling of these distortions is perfectionism: the belief that there's a best solution and that nothing less than the best is acceptable (Antony et al. 1998).

It's not surprising that some people demand perfect solutions. Our problems are real, and it's *essential* that we get the solutions right—right? We need to find *the* solution, the approach that brings only positive outcomes and has no negatives or downsides. Expecting nothing less than the best brings more security and guarantees a positive result, doesn't it?

Actually, it's quite the opposite. Seeking perfect solutions can magnify our anxiety as the future unfolds. Remember lesson 4: the future is uncertain. Because we can't predict how events will present themselves over time, there are no perfect solutions. If events don't develop as planned, you may believe you have failed, which leads to feelings of disappointment and regret and to a reduced sense of efficacy and control. Let's look at a shopping trip to demonstrate how perfectionism can lead to stress and anxiety.

You have three hours to find a new outfit for a very important event, and you need to make a great impression. What kind of shopping trip do you think you'd have if you decided your new clothes had to be dark taupe with a subtle pattern of a contrasting color, made by a particular designer from a silk-wool blend, and offered at a deeply discounted price? On the other hand, you could determine that your new outfit just has to stand out and fit you well. The first scenario would make for a very stressful shopping trip, while the second would offer a much wider range of options and a greater chance for success and satisfaction.

When considering alternative solutions, it helps to allow for some margin of error. Because we can't predict the future, it's important to approach problems flexibly and to accept a positive outcome, not just the perfect one.

So what is a positive or acceptable outcome? It's not perfection, but it's livable. Often you'll find a range of acceptable outcomes. Sometimes half a loaf of bread will do if a full one isn't available. Being open to alternatives and being flexible in what you view as acceptable is the key to remaining hopeful as you confront adversity.

As your perfect plan gives way to a different outcome, you may hesitate and doubt yourself, possibly becoming even less likely to take risks. But a life without risks is a life without reward and growth. So let go of the need to be perfect and to find perfect solutions. You'll get less pressured and less stressed.

KEY POINTS

- When you expect perfection, the only guarantee is that you'll be disappointed.

- Just as you can't predict the future, you can't predict which solution will be the best. You can only make your "best call" given the information you have.

- Being flexible when considering alternative courses of action and seeking "probable solutions" is a healthier way to face the future.

WHAT YOU MAY BE THINKING

But isn't expecting a perfect result just being optimistic? I've always thought, "Make your plan, and then work it." Shouldn't I expect the best?

NOW ASK YOURSELF...

- Can you remember a time when you anticipated a perfect result and it actually happened?

- On the other hand, how often do things turn out a little differently than you expected? How did you feel when you had to live with less-than-perfect results?

- Are there times in which a less-than-perfect outcome turned out to be better in the long run?

WHAT YOU NEED TO DO

1. As you consider alternative solutions to a particular problem, focus on identifying more than one potentially effective solution, rather than searching for a single, perfect solution. Let's try it:

a. Identify a problem that's troubling you now. It doesn't have to be a big one. Any worrisome problem will do.

b. Now list as many possible solutions as you can think of. Don't dismiss any out of hand. Be bold and creative. Think of this process as brainstorming. Write down at least ten to fifteen solutions. Note how you feel. In life, there are a boundless number of directions you can take.

c. Now let's evaluate the solutions. Next to each, jot down its pros and cons, and note its short- and long-term consequences. What are the costs and benefits of each solution?

d. Finally, reflect on the list and assign a "grade" (A, B, C, D, or F) to each; scratch the D's and F's off the list (no need to do something that would be damaging or just wouldn't work).

There you have it—a list of potential solutions!

2. How will you manage if things don't turn out as you plan? Be open to a range of results, and maintain your sense that you are capable of handling a host of outcomes.

3. Although you can't control the future, you can control how you view it. Stay flexible and nimble as you solve life's problems. Adapt.

LESSON 8

SOMETIMES YOU CAN TAKE CONTROL OF BAD SITUATIONS— BUT SOMETIMES NOT

When you have got an elephant by the hind leg and he's trying to run away, it's best to let him run.

—Abraham Lincoln

Very often, when something bad happens, we blame ourselves. We believe we should have seen it coming, and if we did see it coming, we think we should have avoided it or (better yet) prevented it. When we're anxious, fearful, or worried, we often have a heightened sense of responsibility for things we have little or no control over (Rachman 1993). If, for example, you learn that you're about to lose your job, you may find yourself dwelling on whether you could have prevented this. Thoughts such as *Could I have worked harder?* and *Should I have volunteered for that extra assignment?* flow through your mind. Why do we have these kinds of thoughts? Perceiving that we have responsibility implies that we can predict and control events (Salkovskis 1996). By accepting responsibility, we gain a sense of control (and security). But this sense of control comes at a cost: feelings of regret, guilt, and remorse.

This responsibility that we take on allows us to believe that we have greater control over the outcome. It's certainly a reassuring thought: if we just think hard enough about this bad thing, we can *do* something to rectify it. Then we'll feel more secure and be in less danger. Unfortunately, it doesn't always work out this way. The control we're trying to achieve is often unattainable. As a result, we expend mental resources against a situation where we may have little influence. In the process, we rob ourselves of a healthy and constructive mindset, rendering ourselves *less* able to deal with life's problems.

But what about situations where our actions *did* contribute to the problem? To be sure, we all feel remorse for actions we took or didn't take, incorrect decisions, and situations where we acted against our better judgment. How many people now regret applying for a subprime mortgage or an interest-only loan, purchasing a property at the peak of the real-estate market, investing in _____ (any underperforming investment will do), or overextending themselves with a home-equity loan? Looking back, there are always decisions we would have made differently, if only we had known what was ahead. These are life's "woulda, coulda, shoulda's." The question arises: do regret, self-criticism, and self-blame enhance our ability to solve problems going forward? Probably not. While regret may give us pause before we repeat a failed course of action, it doesn't enhance solution-focused thinking (Freeman and DeWolf 1990). With this in mind, applying a touch of self-acceptance and self-forgiveness can help as we learn from our errors.

KEY POINTS

- When a threatening event occurs, determine realistically whether you played a role in causing it and how much influence you have over it in the future.

- Don't take on responsibility for things that are outside your control.

- If you did play a role in causing the problem, take responsibility, be accountable, and learn from your mistake. Then move on. Don't become mired in self-doubt and self-recrimination. Self-acceptance allows you to move forward with greater confidence.

- Recognize that expending your mental resources against situations where you have no influence makes you less capable of dealing with life's challenges.

WHAT YOU MAY BE THINKING

So, I should stop beating myself up? I like that. But what if it is something I caused? You're saying I should just chalk it up as a life lesson and learn from it? It's true—a lot of times I worry about things I really didn't cause. Dwelling on this stuff really changes nothing. But here's the problem for me: I fixate on problems and can't let them go.

NOW ASK YOURSELF...

- Do you blame yourself for situations where you have little or no influence over the outcome? List them.

- What happens to your mental state after you spend time ruminating about a situation over which you have little or no control?

- How does this worry, regret, and blame impact your effectiveness? Does it enhance your performance, perhaps by providing a sense of focus, or does it compromise your effectiveness, gunking up your mind with anxiety-provoking thoughts and images? How does it affect your sense of direction in life and your ability to find solutions?

WHAT YOU NEED TO DO

- Know that viewing yourself as responsible for a situation may not help you cope more effectively with it.

- Ask yourself four questions:

  - Is this problem truly of my making?

  - Are there other people or factors that contributed to the problem? If so, how much of the responsibility for the problem do they bear?

  - How much influence over the situation do I actually have?

  - If I'm not responsible for the problem and I can't control the outcome, will worrying about it help or hinder me?

RECURRING, INTRUSIVE THOUGHTS ARE NORMAL; IT'S THE MEANING WE ATTACH TO THEM THAT COUNTS

*Sitting silently
Doing nothing
Spring comes
And the grass grows by itself.*

—Zen haiku

Everyone has negative thoughts, and lots of them (Rachman and de Silva 1978). Such thoughts and images can be truly upsetting, even shocking. They keep coming back, and we just want them to stop. Most often, anxiety-laden thoughts center on work, grades or academic performance, health, or relationships. But at times, they can include aggressive or violent images, inappropriate or obscene sexual images, or sacrilegious thoughts or ideas. Some people can simply dismiss these thoughts, but for others, it's not that simple—such thoughts and images are graphic, persistent, and disturbing.

Remember the flying monkeys in *The Wizard of Oz?* Negative thoughts are like malicious monkeys that fly through your mind. The types of intrusive, negative thoughts that anxious, worried people experience differ little, however, from the thoughts of nonanxious people. The difference is in the meaning given to the thoughts (Calamari and Janeck 1998). Worried, anxious people often think: *This thought is awful. I shouldn't be thinking this; I have to make it stop.* Of course, the more you focus on the thought and try to make it stop, the faster and more furiously the malicious monkeys fly through your head (Abramowitz, Tolin, and Street 2001). The power to control your distress comes from the ability to disengage from the thought. It is, in a way, paradoxical: you gain control of your thoughts by relinquishing control. Accept them and they will no longer upset you; they may even go away (Marcks and Woods 2005). You need only recognize: *It's just a thought. It means nothing.* So gaze at those evil little monkeys and accept that they have appeared, but know that they aren't real; they're just thoughts. Fly on, little monkeys!

KEY POINTS

1. The first step to dealing with intrusive, negative thoughts is to understand that they are both normal and common.

2. Your brain put those thoughts there, but you don't have to deal with them. You can think of them as you would junk mail, telemarketers, or Internet pop-up ads—they're annoying but unimportant. Disengage from them. Don't dwell on the evil monkeys. Don't tell yourself, "I have to make them stop." Rather, let them be.

3. Allow distressing thoughts to come and go as if they were clouds drifting across the sky or a leaf floating by in a cool summer stream. Don't hold on to them, challenge them, fight against them, or push them away. They're just thoughts.

WHAT YOU MAY BE THINKING

I really want the malicious monkeys to go away. I can't seem to enjoy anything or focus on my work when these thoughts show up. Are you sure this is normal?

NOW ASK YOURSELF...

1. Do you experience recurring, intrusive thoughts? What exactly are they, and why are you afraid of them? After all, they're just thoughts. Can you ignore them?

2. Do you tell yourself you shouldn't think these things? That having such thoughts means there's something wrong with you? That terrible things could happen if you keep thinking this way? That you need to make these thoughts stop? What exactly are your follow-up thoughts? List and evaluate them.

WHAT YOU NEED TO DO

1. Don't be concerned about intrusive negative thoughts. Disengage from them. Accept them. Let them float by. They mean nothing. A thought is just a thought.

2. The secondary cognitions (for example, *I shouldn't be thinking this* and *I have to make it stop*) are a different story. They are the problem. These thoughts aren't true, they potentiate anxiety, and

they should be challenged. When you hear these thoughts in your mind, go after them by writing them down, critiquing them, and determining whether they're true, valid, and helpful. If they aren't, then disregard them. How do you do this? That's coming up in lessons 10 through 14.

LESSON 10

DWELLING ON PROBLEMS IMPAIRS YOUR ABILITY TO COPE

I'm too busy. I have no time for worry.

—Winston Churchill

If you've got a problem, a serious problem, you should think about it, think it through completely—right? Well, maybe.

No matter how intelligent you are, your mind is incapable of thinking about more than a few things at a time. Our brains are a lot like computers: although our long-term memory stores are vast (we come equipped with massive "hard drives"), the amount of material we can focus on at any given time (what fits on the "screen") is comparatively small. The more negative thoughts you have at any given time, the less "attention space" you have to actually solve a problem. It's as if we're filling our computer screens with useless pop-ups.

Allowing negative thoughts to stew in your mind is not a good thing. Whether you call it ruminating, obsessing, or plain old worrying, it just doesn't help. No amount of worrying will give you a better outcome to a bad situation. In fact, it can undo your best intentions.

Going over and over a bad thing that's just happened isn't productive. In fact, it can worsen your anxiety. Beating yourself up and declaring, "This negative thinking has got to stop!" doesn't work either. In fact, you'll probably ruminate about the bad stuff even more (Wells 1995). You need to engage in activities and thinking that clear away the rumination and give your brain a break. What can you do? To refuel your brain, try one of the following:

- Get busy doing something constructive that shows results. Take on a challenging task. Do things that provide a sense of mastery or accomplishment. As you step through the task and feel a sense of mastery, you get a shot of positive emotions in the arm.

- Spend time with friends or family. Don't withdraw. Rather, participate in enjoyable social activities with friends who are understanding and accepting, and can offer fresh perspectives and new ideas for how you might handle the problem.

- Maintain your faith. Spiritual experience, through prayer or meditation, can provide solace from life's tribulations.

KEY POINTS

- Dwelling on problems not only magnifies anxiety but also undermines problem solving.

- When you begin to ruminate or dwell on your problems, take action—do something.

- Refuel your brain by engaging in activities that provide you with feelings of mastery or accomplishment.

- Don't withdraw or isolate yourself from others. Keep in contact with friends and family. Turn to others for support and for fresh ideas and perspectives.

WHAT YOU MAY BE THINKING

Isn't that just escaping? You're telling me to take a break from worrying? Isn't that irresponsible?

NOW ASK YOURSELF...

- Do you allow yourself a break from your fears and anxieties? If so, how do you feel during these breaks? If not, is worrying 24/7 working for you?

- What are the things that give you a true sense of accomplishment when you do them? What are the things that, when you're engrossed in them, put you "in the zone" and provide true satisfaction or, to borrow a term from Mihaly Csikszentmihalyi (1990), give you a sense of "flow"?

- Whom might you turn to for supportive advice? Whom can you turn to for a fresh perspective or a different point of view on your problems?

WHAT YOU NEED TO DO

- Keep in mind that you'll be better able to assess situations realistically and cope effectively when you give your brain a rest. Regularly do things that give you a sense of relief from the pressure; this is a healthy approach when you're solving problems.

- We all need to engage in activities that provide us with a sense of accomplishment. Make a "mastery list" of things you do well and enjoy, and do one or two of the activities on your list each day. Note how doing these things makes you feel.

- When troubled, we all need friends and colleagues who can provide a sense of support and give us new ways of looking at our problems. Talk with at least one person who is supportive and understanding and can offer thoughtful, reflective insights each day.

These activities do more than distract us from rumination; they empower, sustain, and strengthen us. They allow us to develop a clearer and deeper understanding of our lives and possible ways to address our problems.

WORRYING IS HIGHLY OVERRATED

I have been through some terrible things in my life, some of which actually happened.

—Mark Twain

Did you know that most people believe worrying is helpful? Many believe that pondering a problem long enough gives you a better answer, helps you arrive at a better outcome, provides greater insight, or offers you greater confidence in your chosen course of action. They believe worrying helps you avoid problems and stay organized. They view worrying as an effective motivator and feel that it helps you sort out issues. They believe that worrying helps you cope and makes you wiser and more reflective (Borkovec, Hazlett-Stevens, and Diaz 1999).

From this perspective, worrying is a good thing. In fact, it's a *very* good thing. As we've seen, however, excessive worrying can be truly destructive (Davey and Wells 2006). Furthermore, the belief that constant worrying is useful is largely unsupported. It's simply not true.

Two types of worry exist: productive and unproductive. First, let's understand productive worry. If the light on your car's dashboard indicates an empty tank, then your concern about running out of gas is warranted. But if you think for a moment to recall the whereabouts of the closest gas station, go there, and fill the tank, your concern vanishes. Along the same lines, if you forgot to pick up your dog from the groomers and they close in five minutes, a bit of concern is in order. But if you make a call to the groomer, say you're on the way, pick up the dog, and tip more than the usual amount, this worry goes away. In both of these scenarios, worry or anxiety leads to solving the problem by taking effective action. You replace worry with a plan.

But unproductive worry is somewhat different. The worry doesn't lead to an action plan. As a consequence, there's an almost constant twitter of negative, disruptive thoughts. When frequent and compelling, these thoughts can lead to a temporary mental paralysis. Have you ever had days when you just weren't productive, when you couldn't get anything meaningful done, so you just pushed piles around on your desk, had trouble focusing, and felt short tempered? Chances are, you were doing a bit of unproductive worrying. Most worrying touches on one of three areas: work, career, or school performance; health; or relationships—all of which are important concerns. It's natural for us to worry if one of these areas of our lives is threatened.

What can you do? Identify the problem and engage in some solution-focused thinking. Remember, the difference between productive and unproductive worrying is simply whether you can identify a solution. But if there's nothing you can do to solve the problem, disengage from it and let the worrisome thoughts float away.

KEY POINTS

- There are two kinds of worry: productive and unproductive.

- Unproductive worry can be very unpleasant and is accompanied by high levels of anxiety and loss of focus on even simple tasks.

- The difference between productive and unproductive worry is simple. Productive worry results in an action plan, whereas unproductive worry just causes you to mull a problem over without coming to a solution.

- Identify whether or not the problem truly has a solution you can implement. If you do not have any influence or control over the outcome, you have to relinquish control and let the thought "float away."

WHAT YOU MAY BE THINKING

This ruminating and worrying feels uncontrollable. It's really rattling my cage. It just has a life of its own and takes my brain hostage.

NOW ASK YOURSELF...

1. How do you feel when you find yourself worrying unproductively over a situation that has no apparent solution? Come up with five or so words to describe how this makes you feel.

2. What effects, if any, does unproductive worrying have on your relationships with others?

3. Can you remember a time when you identified a solution to a situation and the worrying subsided?

4. Taking this a step further, can you think of a time when you simply let an unproductive worry go and the situation eventually sorted itself out on its own, or a solution presented itself later on?

WHAT YOU NEED TO DO

1. Keep in mind that you can control the worry process. Set aside a specific time period each day to worry (say, 8:00 to 8:30 p.m.). During this period, set your mind against your problems. Write down all of your thoughts and concerns, and allow yourself to reflect, or even dwell, on them. Focus carefully and intently on your problems.

2. Then, at the end of your half-hour reflection period, write down your answer to the following question: what is the solution? You may have several solutions, which is better than just one.

3. Now, set your problems aside. Do something relaxing or enjoyable. Come back to your problems tomorrow at the same time. By taking these steps, you're on your way to channeling your worry into productive, solution-focused thinking. You're also demonstrating to yourself that you control your rumination process. With practice, you can start it and stop it at will.

4. Just remember, for problems where there's no answer or solution, let the problem "float away." No amount of thinking will change a problem over which you have no control or influence.

LESSON 12

DON'T MAGNIFY THE IMPORTANCE OF YOUR PHYSICAL SENSATIONS

The only thing we have to fear is fear itself.

—Franklin D. Roosevelt

Roosevelt's comment on fear has become something of a bromide. Interestingly, he was right. A large body of research indicates that as we become anxious, worried, or fearful, we begin to focus our attention onto our own emotional state.

Researchers refer to this as *self-focused attention* or *anxiety sensitivity*, and it can be a problem (Taylor 1999).

Anxiety sensitivity is the tendency to interpret symptoms of anxiety (things like tension, rapid heartbeat, sweating, and trembling) as indications of a serious physical illness or danger (Reiss and McNally 1985). You begin to think, *Oh no, I could be having a heart attack!* or *I'm going crazy; I could lose it!* Spending your day thinking about what you feel and how awful it is, and carefully attending to your physical sensations, makes your anxiety worse. You feel a bit of tension and anticipate disaster. You then become more anxious, your heart accelerates, and you're off to the races, resulting in a spiral of anxiety, worry, and panic. This spiral can gather quite a bit of destructive momentum, leading to some very unpleasant emotions.

What can you do? Perhaps the best way to cope with these spirals of anxiety is to prevent them altogether. Here are two ways to do this:

- Bring 'em on! Researchers refer to this process as *interoceptive exposure therapy*, and it's really quite simple. Go out and *induce* the physical sensations you fear the most (Clark 1986). Afraid of dizzy sensations? Try spinning in the yard until you feel like tipping over. Afraid of a racing heart? Do some jumping jacks (if your doctor permits). Is light-headedness your trigger? Take some deep breaths (a bit of hyperventilation). By doing this, you can show yourself that the sensations you fear are nothing to be afraid of. They're paper tigers!

- Label your anxious physical sensations. It's almost too simple: you can prevent the spiral by simply naming and describing the symptoms; for example, *Hmmm, there's my heart racing again. So what? Forget it; it's nothing to worry about.*

KEY POINTS

1. If you find that you're becoming sensitive to your physical symptoms of anxiety, that you're vigilant about their showing up and you don't tolerate them well, take action.

2. Keep in mind that these symptoms are innocuous; they don't indicate that something catastrophic is about to happen.

3. Attack the symptoms: induce them and label them. Prove to yourself that these sensations mean nothing!

WHAT YOU MAY BE THINKING

Suppose there's something physically wrong? How do I know I'm not having a heart attack or getting an aneurysm? This sounds risky.

NOW ASK YOURSELF...

- What exactly is it you fear could happen when you experience an otherwise unexplained physical sensation? What's the probability that this event will happen? Is there another way of looking at the situation?

- Could this just be another catastrophic thought? Are you just awfulizing (now with a physical sensation)?

WHAT YOU NEED TO DO

1. Identify the first physical sensation you experience as your anxiety begins to ramp up. What do you notice first? When does this tend to occur? How often have you experienced this in the past? What's the physical symptom you are most concerned about?

2. Are there things that might be causing these sensations other than the catastrophic problem you fear?

3. How might you induce these sensations?

4. If you're comfortable with this approach, give it a try! Induce the worrisome physical sensations. Do it a few times: start them, stop them; start them, stop them. Practice this for a few days and note how you feel. Ask yourself, *Am I as worried about these sensations as I was a week ago?* (You know the answer already: probably not.)

LESSON 13

IT'S TIME TO RELAX

There is more to life than increasing its speed.

—Mohandas Gandhi

It's very hard to be tense, anxious, or worried when you are physically relaxed. As we noted in lesson 1, anxiety and worry *always* imply the presence of a perceived threat. Because you believe danger is present, your body prepares to fight or flee. Your heart rate accelerates, your attention sharpens, the blood flow increases to your arms and legs, your muscles tense, and you're ready for action. But staying wired like this for long periods can be hard on both the body and the spirit.

Moreover, high levels of tension don't promote clear thinking or effective problem solving. It's time to relax.

To relax means to do things that physically release stress and tension. Think of it as a shakedown for your body and brain. Of course, there are many ways to relax. The Rag Doll yoga pose is particularly helpful:

1. Stand with your legs slightly apart and knees bent.

2. Slowly breathe in, drop your chin, and bend at the waist. Now slowly roll your body down.

3. Let your arms dangle. Let them gently sway from side to side. Perhaps shake them a bit. Let your neck and torso relax.

4. After a few seconds, slowly roll back up to a standing position.

Going for a run, a walk, or laps in the pool can also work well. A hot bath or a massage can help, or even a bit of dancing. If nothing else, just stand up in the middle of the room and shake out your tension. Any physical activity that releases physical tension from your body will help.

One of the most effective relaxation methods is simply learning how to breathe. Yes, something as simple as breathing from your abdomen rather than using shallow chest breathing offers a host of benefits to your mind and body. You can do this anywhere: in your car, in a meeting, or even in line at the grocery checkout. It doesn't take planning, time, or a change in your schedule. Try this:

1. Breathe from your abdomen, which means taking a deeper, slower, and fuller breath. Begin by placing your hand on your belly while breathing. If you're taking an abdominal breath, you'll feel your belly, not just your lungs, expand.

2. Inhale slowly while counting to five.

3. Pause and hold your breath for a count of five.

4. Exhale slowly, as if you are cooling a spoonful of hot soup.

5. Follow this with two breaths at normal rhythm.

6. Now repeat the process of deep, slow inhaling and exhaling.

Be careful, though. This is not an exercise in hyperventilation or exaggerated breathing. Often when we feel anxious, our first thought is *Take a deep breath*. But rapidly sucking in a large volume of air can lead to tingling sensations or dizziness, magnifying our anxiety. What's the better approach? Try slow, controlled abdominal breathing.

Another relaxing activity involves guided imagery:

1. Find a quiet place where you won't be interrupted. Lie down or sit in a comfortable chair; either will do.

2. Close your eyes, let your muscles relax, and call to mind a vision of the most peaceful, relaxing place you've ever visited. Perhaps it's a warm tropical beach, whose waves roll up onto the sand, leaving a salty smell in the air. Maybe your relaxing place is a mountain lake where you enjoy the sound of waves lapping against a rocky shore and the feel of a cool breeze blowing through the pines. Your relaxing place can even be something as simple as a lazy Sunday morning in a comfortable bed with overstuffed pillows and a warm down comforter.

3. In your mind, focus closely on what you see, picturing it in detail. What sounds do you hear? Are there any smells? What's the feeling on your skin? Feel the warmth of the sun or the cool crispness of cotton sheets. Take your time and allow the image to develop.

4. Allow your mind to return to this calm, peaceful place. Your feelings of tension will fade as well. It only takes a few minutes.

You need not wait until you feel tense to use these tools. Try them in advance, as a way to prepare for stressful events. The next time you're facing a tough task, a high-powered meeting, a difficult conversation, or any other anxiety-provoking event, try the physical relaxation, controlled breathing, or guided imagery exercise shortly beforehand. You'll feel calmer and more focused.

Anxiety and worry can occur at any time. Often, the things we worry about are days, weeks, months, or even years away. Clinicians refer to this as *anticipatory anxiety*, and it's very common. You can apply these relaxation techniques to this type of anxiety as well. Any time the big "A" takes its cue, try these approaches to calm your mind.

KEY POINTS

- Chronic tension can take a toll on both the mind and the body.

- Physical relaxation (not just distraction from worrisome thoughts) can provide much-needed relief.

- Muscle relaxation, controlled breathing, and guided imagery can bring almost instant relief from feelings of tension and anxiety.

WHAT YOU MAY BE THINKING

This just seems too easy. Dancing, exercise, and even breathing will calm my mind? And only a few minutes of guided imagery will help me feel a sense of calm?

NOW ASK YOURSELF...

- What physical activity or exercise do you find enjoyable? Exercise doesn't necessarily mean the treadmill or heavy physical exertion; it can be as simple as a walk through your neighborhood.

- Everyone has a favorite activity that can be relaxing. Do you enjoy gardening? Taking a long, hot bath? Identify a short list of activities you find calming.

- What's your typical breathing pattern? Do you find that your breathing pattern changes when you're tense, stressed, or worried? Do you tell yourself to take a deep breath when you feel anxious or fearful? How does your body respond to this change in your breathing? Do you begin to experience other physical sensations?

WHAT YOU NEED TO DO

- Practice slow, controlled breathing a few times over the next week, perhaps when you first wake up in the morning or before lunch. Choose times of the day when your routine is fairly predictable, letting the events remind you that it's time to breathe.

- Experiment with the breathing techniques we discussed. Try them out and compare how each of them makes you feel. When you take in a large gulp of air, how do you feel? When you take deep, slow, calm breaths, as previously described, how do you feel?

- Even if you're not a big fan of exercising, build some physical activity into your day. Try parking the car toward the rear of the parking lot and walking briskly to the entrance. Do knee bends while emptying the dishwasher, or simply dance to your favorite song in the kitchen for a minute or two.

- Call to mind a calm, peaceful place, remembering the details. What did you see, feel, smell, and hear? With just a bit of practice, you can train your brain to give your mind a needed break.

LESSON 14

EVALUATE YOUR THOUGHTS AND MAKE THEM ACCOUNT FOR THEMSELVES

There are more things to alarm us than to harm us, and we suffer more often in apprehension than reality.

—Seneca

Approximately eighty years ago, Alfred Adler remarked, "We do not suffer from the shock of our experiences, the so-called trauma, but we make out of them just what suits our purposes. We are self-determined by the meaning we give our experiences. Meanings are not determined by situations, but we determine ourselves by the meanings we give" (1956, 208).

It's true. Different people can have very different reactions to the same situation. It all depends on the meaning we give to it (see Power and Brewin 1997). If we view a problem as intolerable and overwhelming, it will be. If we view the situation as a challenge but a manageable one, it will be. It's all in the way we look at it.

Let me tell you about a previous client named John and a challenge he faced not long ago. He and his family lived in a gorgeous house in an exclusive community. The house was old (it was, in fact, "historical") and quite prominent. He and his family loved the house and loved living there. But financial difficulties hit John's employer, causing his income to drop precipitously. Making matters worse, John's wife lost her job at a local store. No longer able to make the payments on their home, John was forced to put it up for sale and move his family. At the closing table, he was physically sick as he handed the keys to the new owner. The house he and his family had loved was no longer theirs. Recurrent worries and fears rumbled through his mind, keeping him up at night. Would his neighbors and friends see him as a failure? Had he failed at providing for his family? Could the family recover financially? With their reduced family income, how could he pay for his daughter's college? More than just the sale of a house, this move represented the loss of the sense of security he had developed over the years—as he stated, "I feel I've lost everything, like my shirt's been ripped off my back. I just don't know what to do anymore. It's catastrophic."

Managing our thoughts is central to conquering our worries. We discussed the importance of not overestimating the likelihood of negative events or focusing on the worst-case scenario. Now let's go to the next level: the assignment of meaning. If we are truly troubled by something in our lives, it's often because we believe it means something negative about us, that we haven't fulfilled our personal standards and that others will think less of us. We take life's problems, setbacks, and adversities very personally. If our minds are truly troubled by an event, it's important to examine the meanings we've attached to the event.

Let's begin this very important exercise by looking at John's experience in greater detail. Let's examine his thoughts one by one. He perceives he has lost *everything*. His use of the expression "my shirt's been ripped off my back" gives the sense that he feels these events are being unfairly, perhaps maliciously, inflicted on him and that he's powerless to prevent them. He remarks that he doesn't know what to do, reflecting a perceived loss of efficacy or personal ability. Finally, he uses the word "catastrophic." To John this is not just the sale of the house; it's a frightening, horrific life event. But is it? Are these things he's telling himself true? Let's make such thoughts account for themselves before we let them pass.

It helps to be systematic when we examine our thoughts. Begin by thinking about a specific situation or problem that's troubling you. As you reflect on this problem, what are your thoughts? What comes to mind? Write down your thoughts word for word. This is your inner dialogue (what psychologists refer to as *automatic thoughts*), and it can influence how you feel. Ask yourself:

1. What's the thing I most fear will happen?

2. If this happened, what awful thing would it mean about me or my life? Why would this be so terrible?

Next, take a minute to reflect on your answers. Let's treat our thoughts as objects to be examined, not statements of fact. Define your terms. What exactly do these words mean? While it can help to look up their definitions in a dictionary, we're also interested in what the words mean to you. What are your *personal* definitions? John's thoughts include words such as "failure," "lost," and "everything." What exactly is the definition of "failure," and does he meet the criteria? What about "everything"? Did he actually lose "everything"? Do your worrisome thoughts contain adverbs like "always" and "never," or magnifying adjectives such as "terrible," "horrific," "devastating," "intolerable," and "unacceptable"? John views his predicament as "catastrophic." What exactly does this mean, and is it true? Words often associated with "catastrophe" include "disaster," "tragedy," "calamity," and "ruin." Is that what has happened in his life?

At times the essential source of our fears and worries isn't entirely clear. We know something is truly troubling us, but we have difficulty putting our finger on it. For John it's not about the house (he's lived in quite a few places during his life, and they've all been fine), and it's not about his daughter's college (he knows she'll get through). So what is it? Here, a technique called the "downward arrow" (Wright, Basco, and Thase 2006) can be helpful. Take a piece of paper and draw an arrow down the left side. At the top of the page, write down your most upsetting thought. When we ask John, he responds, "It's the feeling that I've been swept into an avalanche that's headed down a mountain. We'll never recover."

In understanding the meaning of this statement, we begin by asking, "And this would be a terrible thing because it means what? What's the first thing that comes to your mind?"

He responds, "This is just unstoppable. We'll never have a sense of security."

This is followed by the same question: "And this would be a terrible thing because it means what?" Each automatic thought elicited is followed by the same question. By repeating this process, we develop a list of worrisome thoughts, each more negative and troubling than the last. From this list, an underlying theme emerges, representing the truly worrisome thought. Here's John's downward arrow:

1. I've been swept into an avalanche heading down a mountain.

2. We'll never recover.

3. This is just unstoppable.

4. We'll never have a sense of security.

5. I'm not providing for my family.

6. Caring for his family is the most important thing a man can do.

7. It means I'm not measuring up. I'm a failure.

8. My life's meaningless; it's been a waste.

9. All my efforts mean nothing.

As we can see, this is about far more than the sale of a house. When asked if he hears a theme in all of this, John replies, "Sure, it's about providing for your family," and he begins to describe his experiences as a child, when his father lost his job and the family was forced to move. For John, this was revisiting a terrible memory. It meant he wasn't measuring up. Here we have the real issue, the thing John *truly* fears. The question arises, Is this true? Let's also make this thought account for itself. The next lesson covers this topic.

WHAT YOU MAY BE THINKING

There are so many of these thoughts floating through my mind. If it's not one thing, it's another. How do I know which one is most important? By the way, when I think about this stuff, I feel worse. Won't reflecting on these things just make me more anxious?

NOW ASK YOURSELF...

1. Can you identify the thoughts that accompany your feelings of anxiety?

2. Are there specific thoughts or issues that are more troubling than others?

WHAT YOU NEED TO DO

1. Think about the situation or problem that troubles you the most. As you reflect on this problem, what are your thoughts? Write them down, word for word.

2. Now, let's tease those words apart. Define your terms. Are there magnifying adverbs or adjectives?

3. Try the downward arrow. Start with the most distressing automatic thought and ask yourself, "This would be a terrible thing, an awful thing, because it means what?" Repeat the questioning, writing down the first thought that comes to your mind. Does a theme or underlying concern appear? Does a core fear rise to the surface?

CHANGING YOUR THOUGHTS

Man can alter his life by altering his thinking.

—William James

You've now identified your negative automatic thoughts, the troubling worries that flicker and flash through your mind, and the underlying core fears. As we've seen, these thoughts often center on themes of vulnerability, insecurity, personal inability, or weakness, and they often carry a sense that we haven't measured up to our personal standards or expectations. These thoughts are truly upsetting, and we really believe them. But are they true, and are they adaptive? That is, do they help or hinder us? Let's find out. Let's put them to the test. Once you have identified the central component of your anxiety, write down your answers to the following four questions:

1. What's the evidence for and against this belief? The evidence may be very apparent, or you may have to dig for it. Be as hyperlogical as you can. Be objective and thorough.

   John, for example, believes that having had to sell his house demonstrates that he doesn't "measure up" and "can't provide" for his family. Let's look at the evidence for and against this:

Evidence For	Evidence Against
In this culture, having a good job is a hallmark of success.	I've been successful at other jobs in the past, so I'm not some loser who's incapable of success.
Lots of my friends from college, even my brother, are earning a lot more than I do.	I've got a good skill set, and I work very hard at what I do. That never changes.
This was a big financial loss. We don't have the financial security we did even a few months ago.	These cutbacks at work weren't about me; I was doing fine. They affected everyone in our department.

	I'm still providing the essentials for my family. We still have a house and food, and our kids are still healthy and doing well in school.
	Nobody has said I'm a loser or that I need to get my act together—quite the opposite; everyone has been supportive and understanding.
	I've been through worse before. They don't call it an economic cycle for nothing. As they say about boxers, "It's not whether you get knocked down; it's whether you get back up that's important."

2. Is there another way of looking at this? Most often the evidence is mixed—some pro, some con. What do you make of this? Is there a hidden opportunity in this bad event? Sometimes our lives get a bit of a shake-up, and something very good can come of it. Is there another side to this story?

   For John, the evidence is mixed. Some of the evidence is consistent with his belief that he doesn't "measure up," but a good deal of the evidence is not. Taken together, the evidence from his life doesn't demonstrate that he is incapable and "can't provide" for his family. Quite the opposite—he addressed his family's financial problems directly and effectively: his family was able to "downsize" and is quite secure with a smaller mortgage and lower expenses. John may want to consider other avenues for success, such as finding a better job or devoting himself to a long-held dream or aspiration he hasn't had time for. At the same time, this situation may lead him to reconsider the importance he has attached to possessions (for example, living in a prominent, "historical" house was an indicator of his value or worth). The move may also offer an opportunity to demonstrate to his children (and himself) the value of being resilient in the face of adversity or of having a more accepting attitude toward human frailty and insecurity (sometimes, as much as we'd like to, we can't provide everything we want for those we care for). You can argue that some personal strengths only become apparent in challenging times and that growth comes from adversity.

3. So what? If your fears are true, is this fact truly important for your future? It's important to keep problems, losses, and setbacks in perspective. Don't magnify their significance. If your most

feared event did occur, would it still be a problem in a year? In five years?

4. So? What action are you going to take to resolve this problem? What can you do to stop the feared event from happening? What's the solution? Solution-focused thinking is far more helpful than rumination. What are your choices? Brainstorm and come up with a list of ten or more different courses of action directed toward either making sure the feared event doesn't happen or making it less significant if it does. Be creative in generating your list. What are the pros and cons of each action? Which courses of action do you choose? What are the necessary steps? Are you confident in your ability to take these steps? If not, what do you need?

What if the event you fear does, in fact, come to pass? The storm you saw in the distance has come ashore in your life. The same strategies—rationally and dispassionately examining your thoughts about the event, keeping the event in perspective, developing more adaptive ways of thinking about the situation, applying solution-focused thinking, actively solving the problem, and developing social support—can all be brought into play. At the same time, it can help to accept hardship as an integral part of life and a pathway to growth.

As you recall, anxiety stems from perceiving a threat: something dangerous is coming your way. You can direct solution-focused thinking toward making sure the feared event doesn't occur or toward coping with the situation as it evolves. To be sure, it can be more difficult to develop effective solutions when the threat is symbolic or based on a judgment (for example, "My life's meaningless" or "I'm not measuring up"). But even here, you can step back, evaluate the thought, and chart a course of action. If your life feels meaningless, what can you do? What actions can you take that will give your life a sense of meaning, value, and purpose?

Now, set aside the list, the questions, and your answers. Give your mind a rest. Do something enjoyable, such as visiting friends or doing something that gives you a sense of accomplishment. Begin to refuel your mind. The things you need to know are on your list and you've made a plan. Come back to the list after a break, and reflect. How would you like to proceed in the situation you've been considering? Cognitive-behavioral clinicians refer to the previous types of questions as *rational responding, cognitive restructuring,* or simply *evaluating the evidence*, and they are powerful tools for managing anxiety, worry, hopelessness, and depression (Wright, Basco, and Thase 2006). With practice, changing the way you view yourself and your world can remake your life.

KEY POINTS

- The meanings we give to life experiences determine our emotional reaction and how we respond.

- It's important to clarify what these distressing thoughts are and evaluate them systematically. Make your beliefs, attitudes, thoughts, and expectations account for themselves. Are they true? Are they consistent with the evidence of your life? Is it reasonable and helpful to look at things this way? Is there another way of looking at things?

WHAT YOU MAY BE THINKING

I've always thought of my thoughts as sound and sensible. If I really believe something, it must be true. At least, I'm pretty sure it's true. Does this mean my thoughts are irrational? I try to be reasonable; my way of thinking about problems seems sensible to me.

NOW ASK YOURSELF...

- Does writing down the problem and the associated thoughts help you focus? Does it bring greater clarity to the issue?

- Is there a downside to reflecting on your thoughts and to evaluating whether your inner voice is sensible?

WHAT YOU NEED TO DO

1. Get it on paper. Think about the situations and problems that trouble you the most. Write down your thoughts. Which thoughts are the most distressing?

2. Now, evaluate the thoughts you've written down. Make them account for themselves. Critically evaluate them using the four questions. Are these thoughts reasonable? Are you being rational in your judgments? Is there another way of looking at the situation? (As one of my professors once quipped, "There are an infinite number of interpretations for any given observation.") Are you keeping the situation in perspective? What's the solution?

3. Finally, let's begin to move from thought to action. Let's make a plan. What can you do? Write down the steps you would like to take to avoid the potential problem or to cope with it. Be specific and concrete. When would you like to get started at putting your solutions into action? Are there obstacles you'll need to address? How would you like to manage them?

LESSON 16

WHEN YOU'RE WORRIED OR ANXIOUS, AVOIDING PROBLEMS IS AMONG THE WORST THINGS YOU CAN DO

You gain strength, courage, and confidence by every experience in which you really stop to look fear in the face. You are able to say to yourself, "I have lived through this horror; I can take the next thing that comes along." You must do the thing you think you cannot do.

—Eleanor Roosevelt

As we have seen, anxiety and worry indicate that we perceive a threat. If we see danger coming, our natural reaction is to get away, avoid the trouble. If you hear footsteps behind you on a dark night on a deserted street, your anxiety level rises and you quicken your pace to get away. You move to the other side of the street to avoid the threat. If your boss asks you to give a presentation to the senior management of your company, your anxiety builds from the fear you won't do well, and you try to find a way to get out of it (or to, at least, avoid thinking about it). Anxiety and avoidance influence our lives in myriad ways, large and small. Some people avoid calling clients; others avoid discussing difficult things with their spouses or opening credit-card statements. All too many people avoid going to the dentist. In all of these cases, as you evade the threat, your anxiety declines. This reduction in anxiety level has two consequences: First, it reinforces the avoidant behavior; you'll be more likely to skitter away from alleys and avoid presentations in the future. Second, it reinforces the belief that there really was a threat and that you really couldn't cope (Freeman et al. 1990). With every experience in which we dodge a danger rather than confront it, we come to feel more vulnerable and view ourselves as less capable. What's the take-home lesson? Avoidance itself is the problem. Avoidance reinforces the belief that there really was a threat and that you could only manage it by avoiding the situation.

Paradoxically, the way to overcome anxiety and worry is to *approach* the things we fear. If you have a fear of dogs, sooner or later you'll have to pet some puppies. If you have a fear of flying, you'll have to get on an airplane. Afraid of public speaking? Begin by giving a presentation to a small, friendly audience. If you're afraid of the thin envelope from the collection agency, you'll have to open it. Interestingly, the results of a series of surveys completed by Freddie Mac and Roper Public Affairs and Media (Freddie Mac 2008) indicate that many home owners who are delinquent on their mortgage payments never call their lenders to ask for help. They receive a delinquency or foreclosure notice and freeze; they aren't aware of possible solutions and don't think anything will help. As a result, they set the notice aside—they don't want to think about it. With this in mind, when you're dealing with anxiety and avoidance, the three most important words are "exposure, exposure, exposure." Put simply, that which you fear is what you should do, or as Eleanor Roosevelt said, "You must do the thing you think you cannot do."

Let's think carefully about this. The most important part of the previous sentence is "do." Take action; address the problem directly. Behavioral psychologists often recommend *systematic desensitization*, or *graded exposure*, as a means of overcoming anxiety (Wolpe 1982). Let me explain what this means; it's intuitively sensible. For each fear (for example, the fear of dogs), make a list of ten to twelve anxiety-provoking situations, arranging them in order of severity (start with the easiest, such as being in the same room with a golden retriever puppy, and finish with the most difficult, such as petting your friend's hundred-pound Doberman), and then approach each in turn. Start with the simplest, approaching each situation slowly. Stay with it until you are *entirely* calm and comfortable, and then move to the next level. You will gain confidence as you proceed. Through this graduated approach, you can overcome virtually any fear. The key is to take action. Never avoid. If you're doing something, you are taking one step toward dealing with the source of your worry. If you're actively working on a solution, you're not avoiding the problem. Problems? Bring them on! Our dictum? Exposure, exposure, exposure!

To be sure, some fears *are* reasonable and some avoidance makes sense. It's smart to run out of a burning building. It's reasonable to step away from a snarling pit bull. But these are not our primary concern. Avoidance becomes a problem when the anxiety-provoking stimulus is relatively innocuous (for example, petting a Chihuahua, answering the doorbell, or opening the mail) or the consequences of avoidance are high (for example, not responding to a foreclosure notice, not having that unexplained growth on your neck checked out, or not calling clients at work). In these situations, it makes sense to take steps to manage the anxiety and avoidance.

KEY POINTS

- Despite offering momentary relief, avoiding problems and withdrawing from stressors typically exacerbate life's problems.

- Avoidance and withdrawal have several consequences: they reinforce the belief that the problem really was overwhelming and unmanageable, they solidify the belief that you really are weak and unable to cope, and they deprive you of the opportunity to practice coping skills and to develop feelings of control, competence, and efficacy.

- Remember, what we fear doing is what we should do. Bring it on!

WHAT YOU MAY BE THINKING

So the key to overcoming a fear is to face it, head on? Isn't that dangerous? Besides, some of these fears are reasonable. If someone is coming out of a dark alley at night, I'm gonna run. That's the wise thing to do. When there's a snarling dog—I don't care how large—I'll try to back away. It just seems sensible. How can I know if my avoiding things is healthy or unhealthy? It seems subjective.

NOW ASK YOURSELF...

- How does your fear limit you? For instance, if you're afraid of snakes, will you forgo the family camping trip? Is avoiding calls at the office affecting your work performance?

- Are there situations or problems you are avoiding that might have more serious consequences (such as opening a letter from a collection agency, a foreclosure notice, or the results of a medical test or procedure)? What thoughts and feelings do you have while reflecting on this situation?

- Do you feel trapped by your fear? Is it controlling your behavior and your life plans? How?

WHAT YOU NEED TO DO

1. Right now, note what you tend to avoid by making a brief list. Are there one or two challenges or problems you want to avoid the most?

2. What emotions do you have as you think about these problems? What thoughts go through your mind? Stay with them. Don't try to push them out of your mind. Write down your thoughts and feelings.

3. Now, let's take action. What initial small steps would be helpful in approaching these problems? What do you need to do? What resources or supports would help as you begin to address the problem? When would you like to start? (There's no time like the present!)

4. As you approach problems rather than avoid them, how do you feel? Do you notice any changes in your thoughts about the problems? Are there changes in the emotions you have when you think about them? By approaching problems rather than avoiding them, you may be able to change how you perceive them and gain a greater sense of confidence.

LESSON 17

SOCIAL ANXIETY: WORRYING TOO MUCH ABOUT WHAT OTHERS THINK

Nothing so much prevents our being natural as the desire to seem so.

—François de La Rochefoucauld (1678)

The above epigraph was written over three hundred years ago and is still true today. The thing that keeps us from feeling relaxed and comfortable, or natural, in social situations is our desire to impress others. Our anxiety can often spill over into our social lives in unexpected ways. Not everyone experiences *social anxiety*, but it is quite common and deserves some discussion.

Several years ago I had the opportunity to sit in on a meeting of upper level managers of a Fortune 500 company. Well over two hundred attendees were in the room, and the purpose of the meeting was to introduce the new executive vice president. It was a sea of suits, properly polished shoes, and overall impeccable attire. The atmosphere was tense. All were waiting for the new boss to come and speak.

When he arrived, it was nothing like what anyone had expected. He approached the lectern and, rather than stand behind it with his hands bracing each side, he leaned against the side of it. As the spotlight followed him across the stage, it became apparent that he had no notes! He was simply going to talk to the group. Although he wore a suit, his tie was a bit loose. What was his opening? "Hey, how are you today?" The audience instantly liked this man. He broke every rule of formal public speaking and, at the same time, broke down all the walls. It was a most amazing exhibition of self-confidence and social poise. The executive made the meeting about the audience, not about impressing others or establishing his authority.

What was his greatest strength? Although he was well prepared, he wasn't focused on what people thought of him.

Rather, he was focused on learning about them. He had a sincere interest in the employees and their work. He was natural.

Social anxiety is normal and very common. We all want to be liked, loved, respected, admired, and treated kindly. But sometimes we want it too much. We want to manage what others think of us, and we view criticism or (even worse) rejection as intolerable. To be sure, we each have times when our confidence is a bit tested or we don't feel on top of our game. But for many people, virtually any social situation is fraught with danger. They feel that they don't measure up, and they're constantly vigilant for signs that others disapprove (for example, "I saw that yawn," "He looked away while I was talking," or "She stopped smiling when I came in the room"). As the anxiety builds, they begin to monitor their own behavior, lest they say or do something inappropriate (for example, "My hand is shaking, and there's a drop of sweat on my forehead; people will notice"). That's a lot of thinking, monitoring, and feeling anxious. How exhausting!

When we're consumed this way, we aren't part of the party or function. Rather, worry and discomfort hold us hostage. When you become fixated on how you are coming across, feel as if you are onstage, view others as potentially critical, and feel that there are standards you just can't reach, it's very hard to feel natural and be at ease (Clark and Wells 1995).

What can you do? The best approach has two components: rational responding (from lesson 15) and exposure (from lessons 12 and 16). Begin by noting and evaluating the thoughts you have during social situations. What's going through your mind? What do you fear could happen? As you attend to your thoughts, do you notice any cognitive distortions (Freeman et al. 1990)? Do you, for example, tend to awfulize the situation, overgeneralize (for example, see a time-limited problem as lasting forever), magnify (for example, focus on signs of danger or risk while overlooking reassuring aspects of the situation), or try to read minds to see what others are thinking about you? If so, challenge these thoughts and consider whether there might be another way of thinking about the situation.

Many people find it helpful to develop adaptive self-statements—mantras, for lack of a better term—they can repeat to themselves. Examples are, "I've been in situations like this a hundred times before," "This is a home audience; the folks here like me," and "This should be fine; every new person I meet is a potential new friend." As you gain a sense of control over the anxious thoughts, it's time to take on some social settings (Hope et al. 2000).

Begin by making a list of eight to ten anxiety-laden social situations. The situations and tasks should be related and should provide you with opportunities to disprove your fearful expectations (that is, they should show you that you had nothing to fear and that you had the ability to handle the situation comfortably). A sample list follows. Start with a situation that's not at all anxiety provoking, and slowly begin to take on situations that are challenging but not overwhelming. As you encounter a situation, note your negative thoughts and challenge them. Relax and focus on the adaptive self-statements. Stay with the situation until you are entirely relaxed. Don't just endure the situation—take a moment to *enjoy* the social encounter. Stay with it until your anxiety all but entirely dissipates.

- Sitting in a public park

- Talking with a new acquaintance outside of work

- Talking with a coworker

- Eating in the company cafeteria and talking with a group

- Introducing yourself to a stranger at the office

- Talking privately with your boss

- Asking a question in an office meeting

- Making a formal presentation to your department

Once you're comfortable with a situation, move to the next one on your list. Repeat this process with each scenario until they're all easy. Now you're a natural!

KEY POINTS

- Anxiety in social situations is common and normal.

- As with any anxiety, you can overcome social anxiety by changing your thoughts and practicing new behaviors.

WHAT YOU MAY BE THINKING

Worry about what people think? Of course I do. It's important what others think. I want people to think well of me and respect me. Who wouldn't?

NOW ASK YOURSELF...

- Do you feel anxious or uncomfortable in social situations? Is your anxiety so high that you want to avoid the situation or that you really don't want to go out?

- It's a leading question, but let's ask it anyway: is it even possible to have everyone like, admire, and respect you? Probably not. With this in mind, can you accept that there are some people who won't accept, like, or respect you without this leading you to feel anxious and bad about yourself?

WHAT YOU NEED TO DO

1. Though fairly straightforward, overcoming social anxieties requires a systematic approach that addresses all three components of anxiety—your thoughts, physical sensations, and behaviors. With this in mind, take out your notepad, and let's tease apart your reactions in social situations:

    a. What thoughts go through your mind when you're in a social situation? Do you feel self-conscious?

    b. What physical sensations do you experience at those times? Does your heart race? Do you shake or sweat? How noticeable are these symptoms? If people noticed them, what would they think?

    c. Do you change your behavior when you're around others? Are there things you avoid?

2. Let's begin by addressing the negative thoughts. What's the evidence that people are looking at you, thinking less of you, or criticizing you? Is there another way to look at this?

3. Now, let's take some social action. Make your list of anxiety-laden social situations. Start by approaching the easiest situation. Give it a try.

LESSON 18

WHAT'S REALLY ON YOUR MIND?

Worry gives a small thing a big shadow.

—Swedish proverb

I'm out of dog food. The dog seems sluggish lately. I wonder if he's getting old. He's eight; he's getting up there. Maybe he has cancer! What would I do if my dog died? You know, I've been on hold for twenty minutes with this insurance company. No one seems to be able to find the right information to approve this

*physical therapy bill. The whole day has been this way.
I knew when I woke up this morning it was going to
be this way. It all started when the coffee carafe broke.
Now I can't find my gold bracelet. It was my mother's
and it means everything to me. What if I lost it? I'm
always losing everything!—like my favorite umbrella; I
lost that on the train last week. I'll never find another
umbrella like that one.*

Jane is having a rough day. All of these thoughts keep
cascading through her mind; it's exhausting, just one problem
after another. As you can see, Jane has a slew of worries going
through her brain, wearing her down, and making her feel
worse by the minute. Ever have a day like this? What can
you do?

As you recall from lesson 1, anxiety always implies the
presence of a perceived threat. Something bad is about to
happen and we don't like it. We want to avoid it. If the threat
is a bug or high places, we call it a phobia; if it's speaking or
performing in public, we call it social anxiety; if it's a physical
sensation—well, that can lead to feelings of panic. But what
happens if *everything* makes us anxious? When this happens,
we tend to feel vulnerable, tense, and apprehensive virtually
all the time. Our concerns are diffuse, and life just feels overwhelming. That's what's happening with Jane.

Now, let's look at each of Jane's worrisome thoughts: She
needs dog food. The dog is sleeping a lot. So does every other
bored dog in town. The dog needs a walk. Being on hold with
an insurance company isn't something to get upset about; it
happens to everyone. There's nothing that says a broken cof-

feepot means her whole day will be bad. In fact, it gives her an excuse to buy that new model she's had her eye on. Finally, she can buy a new umbrella, and while she's at it, she should buy a few since we all lose umbrellas. What about the gold bracelet? Okay, now we're on to something. Jane's mother passed away two weeks ago, after a long battle with cancer. There you have it.

Now, ask yourself: What's *really* on your mind? While your mind is actively engaged in the art of worrying, it becomes something of a robot, processing, ruminating, and sorting through files and files of information, experiences, and beliefs. Focusing on small details or annoyances is really just a form of avoidance. In this case, it's cognitive avoidance. It protects us from having to think about the problem that's truly threatening, the thing we *really* fear. What's truly painful or frightening is just below the surface, and by thinking about a lost umbrella or a broken carafe, we don't have to address the real problem. In Jane's situation, all her worry twitters had a theme of loss. What if the dog died? Will she never have another umbrella she likes as much as the one she lost? Then there's the broken coffeepot and, finally, the lost gold bracelet. But the true threat is much larger: the loss of her mother.

Anxiety comes when we feel threatened. Sure, we can distract ourselves with tasks and chores, or redirect our thoughts to minor problems, but the big threat is still there. We may not want to think about it, but it's there. The real problem has just gone underground, in the mind's tunnels. Oh, it's there, simmering away, waiting for its turn to come forward.

So while you worry about minor annoyances, the really upsetting thing is temporarily at bay. Unfortunately, focusing on minor problems renders us less able to cope with the true problem, the true source of our anxiety. But we can only do so much, handle so much. When there's a major source of anxiety in your life, strive to make it a priority. Put the focus of your attention where it belongs, on the real problem, not on minor issues that use up your coping resources.

In Jane's case, she needs to recognize that she's going through a period of mourning and to focus on her grief and on living her days without her mother. What's the cure? Have a good think. This is thinking at its best: rational, methodical, and solution focused. At the same time, you need to feel. Let yourself reflect on the real problem, the thing you truly fear, and *feel* the emotions that accompany it. This may be an unpleasant experience. You may feel sad, despondent, ashamed, lonely, angry, hopeless, or frightened. But the only way to deal with the feelings is to begin to feel them. Don't avoid these fears and their accompanying feelings. Let them out and let them be. Be constructive and generate solutions. Manage the thing you really fear.

KEY POINTS

- Generalized anxiety—worrying about a wide range of problems—may stem from a general sense of personal vulnerability; the world seems like a dangerous place in many ways.

- Worrying about a large number of minor problems can serve a function. It can serve as a form of cognitive avoidance, protecting us from the anxiety that accompanies reflecting on larger problems and issues that are truly frightening.

- The best way to cope is to cut to the chase: Ask, "What's the real thing I'm worried about? How can I manage this?" Don't avoid it. Take it on.

WHAT YOU MAY BE THINKING

This is frightening. I've got so much to think about, so many worries every day, and you're telling me to go after the big one. I know it's there, but it's huge. It has to do with _____.

NOW ASK YOURSELF...

- Do I tend to have a lot of minor, seemingly unrelated worries, or is there one thing that's really troubling me?

- If I weren't worried about all these little things—if I set them all aside—what would I worry about?

WHAT YOU NEED TO DO

1. Try an experiment: Give up worrying about little things for thirty minutes. Let the thoughts go. Relax and reflect. During this period, what thoughts come to your mind? Do larger concerns, worries, or fears emerge? If there's a larger concern, let's shine some light on it.

2. On a piece of paper, jot down your thoughts about this concern. Why is it significant? What does it mean about you and your life?

3. In lesson 14 we discussed the downward arrow. Take the most upsetting thought you have about this problem and apply the downward arrow to it. Does a core fear emerge? If yes, let's apply the four questions (from lesson 15) to it. If no core fear is apparent, apply the four questions to the initial distressing thought.

4. Many times, core fears have developed over long periods of time. Many people recall having had these thoughts and fears when they were quite young. They report, "I've always felt this way." When is the earliest you can recall having had this core fear and its accompanying thoughts and beliefs?

5. On one side of a sheet of paper, list all the experiences you've had over the years that support these beliefs and feelings. Take your time and be comprehensive.

6. Now, flip the sheet over and list all the experiences you've had during your life that are inconsistent with your core fear. As you compare the two lists, what comes to mind? Is there another way of thinking about your core fear? Can you reframe it?

FLOW WITH THE CURRENT OF LIFE

By letting it go, it all gets done.... But when you try and try, the world is beyond winning.

—Lao-tzu

Lao-tzu was quite right. Let me explain why. If you've ever been white-water rafting, you know that one of the first lessons you learn is this: If you're thrown from the raft (and at some point you *will* be), wrap your hands up around your head (protect what's most important), aim your feet downstream, and be like a stick. Relinquish control and let the current carry your body through the rapids. Eventually the currents will carry you to a calm eddy. But if you fight the current, you'll expend needless energy and hit the rocks. Pain will ensue.

So it is with life. Sometimes very difficult situations have no simple answers, so we have to let the current of life carry us along. This brings us back to lesson 4, on the importance of accepting ambiguity and of maintaining faith and optimism in the face of adversity. As Thomas Aquinas said, "Faith has to do with acceptance of things not seen, and hope with things not at hand."

Let's consider Benjamin Franklin's take on life. He remarked, "Our limited perspective, our hopes and fears, become our measure of life, and when circumstances don't fit our ideas, they become our difficulties." Many times, we are confronted by events that "don't fit our ideas." Here is where acceptance and hope are most important (Orsillo and Roemer 2005).

A friend of mine, Allie, who recently passed away, had been blind since contracting an illness at the age of three. That was in 1923, and during those times, a child with a disability this severe was often institutionalized for life. Thank goodness for Allie's forward-thinking parents, who reassured her, "You will find your way." Allie went on to become a happily married concert pianist and to raise four children. When asked about being blind, she responded, "It is a major inconvenience."

There are many Allies in the world, and they teach us a most important lesson: Remain steadfast in the face of adversity. Accept life's challenges as well as its gifts.

KEY POINTS

- When you're confronted by a serious problem you have no control over, the wise approach is to flow with the current.

- Keeping an open mind as life reveals itself is the key to finding calm after the storm.

- Recognize the difficulties and inconveniences, but also recognize the gifts in life.

WHAT YOU MAY BE THINKING

Go with the flow? I've heard that before. It's a lot easier said than done. By the way, what does it really mean? Are you telling me to act like I don't care when bad things happen? Even worse, does this mean I shouldn't complain?

NOW ASK YOURSELF...

- Were there situations in the past where you wish you'd been able to maintain a sense of composure in the face of a threat? Are there problems in your life now where adopting this stance, allowing events to evolve, would be helpful?

- Following the example of the white-water rafter, what does it mean in your life to cover your head and protect what's most important?

WHAT YOU NEED TO DO

1. Make a list of the three or four most difficult situations in your life, the things you worry about the most. Which of them could you fix with effort? Which of them (like Allie's blindness) can't be fixed?

2. How would your thoughts and behavior change if you were to accept this predicament? What's the "calm eddy" you hope to reach? That is, what positive outcome might you be able to bring about?

LESSON 20

LIVE WISELY

To conquer fear is the beginning of wisdom.

—Bertrand Russell

We all have heard the serenity prayer: "God grant me the serenity to accept the things I cannot change, the courage to change the things I can, and the wisdom to know the difference." These are, indeed, wise words. They fit beautifully with our understanding of anxiety and worry: both acceptance and thoughtful action play a role in how we manage life's struggles.

"… and the wisdom to know the difference" is the key phrase. But what *is* wisdom, and how do we develop it? Philosophers and theologians have thought about this for ages and have proposed a large number of theories about what wisdom is and how it develops. More recently, evolutionary biologists, psychologists, and social neuroscientists have begun to work on the question (Sternberg and Jordan 2005). In the broadest sense, wisdom entails the judicious use of knowledge, thoughtful and pragmatic decision making, compassion, self-reflection, insight, open-mindedness, altruism, tolerance for others, and maintaining a sense of emotional balance and calm in the face of stress (Meeks and Jeste 2009). It can also entail approaching problematic situations creatively and constructively, while resisting situational or social pressures.

Wisdom is a trait and a virtue that all of us can have. It's not a rare attribute, and it's not something you either have or don't have. Rather, you can cultivate it and nurture it. You start this process in reflection, by asking the prudent question and by broadening your perspective by considering others' interests and long-term outcomes. Both a kind of knowledge and a way of thinking, wisdom is acquired and molded through life experience.

When you're confronted by a problem, it's easy to take it personally. But it can help to step back and take the broad view: *How can I promote the common good and rise above personal interests? What are the perspectives of others involved? How does the problem affect them? How do they feel? In tackling this problem, are there ways I can empathically and compassionately support others? In this difficult situation, is there an opportunity for altruism and cooperation?*

While you're looking for practical solutions, it can help to consider whether there are other ways or levels at which you can understand the problem. What does the situation tell you about the complexities of human nature and social relationships? Are there broader ethical issues at play? Wisely responding to problems requires us to pause, to restrain ourselves from responding immediately based on our emotions and to hesitate before making an ethical decision in a utilitarian way.

Maintaining a sense of calm balance in the face of adversity is central to responding wisely. Controlling your negative emotions and impulses is important, as is cultivating the ability to maintain positive emotions such as gratitude, caring, and happiness in times of strife. Show appreciation for others. Put your negative feelings into words and reframe them before expressing them.

Be tolerant of your fellow humans, their foibles, and their shortcomings. We are all flawed and misguided, and we all make mistakes. Keep in mind that others may not see the world (or the problem) the same way you do. Be open to the possibility of alternative perspectives or viewpoints.

Wisdom is a wonderful human attribute that greatly aids us in responding to life's travails. It's a virtue we can develop with practice.

KEY POINTS

- Wisdom is a virtue you can develop.

- Because wisdom provides a sense of perspective to life's challenges, it reduces worry and fear.

- Wisdom contains several components—knowledge, self-reflection, tolerance, patience, compassion, wonder and open-mindedness, empathy, and emotional balance—all of which you can nurture within yourself.

WHAT YOU MAY BE THINKING

Well, what does wisdom have to do with worrying? This is getting really abstract. I thought this was just a little book with tips for coping with fear and anxiety. Will this help me stop worrying about my bills? But you know, I like the idea of living wisely— this could change who I am as a person.

NOW ASK YOURSELF...

- Are there situations in the past where you've shown wisdom?

- Whom do you view as thoughtful and wise? How does that person manage difficult, challenging situations? Is this an approach you would like to model or emulate?

WHAT YOU NEED TO DO

1. Make a list of people you know who show the characteristics of wisdom. Now, think of a specific problem or concern in your life. How would these people approach it?

2. Wisdom is composed of several characteristics: practical knowledge, self-reflection, tolerance, patience, compassion and acceptance of others, wonder and open-mindedness, sensitivity to moral and ethical issues, independence of thought, empathy, and emotional balance. List these on a sheet of paper and ask yourself, "How would I rate my behavior in each of these dimensions?" Next to each, jot down situations where you've shown this characteristic in the past. How did you behave, think, and feel in this situation? (As you can see, you are self-monitoring your wise actions).

3. Finally, let's apply this process to a problem that worries you now. Step through each of the characteristics and ask, "How can I apply this to my current situation? How can I approach this problem wisely?"

EPILOGUE:
A FINAL NOTE

Life can be hard. Fear, anxiety, and worry stem from feelings of vulnerability and are magnified by a loss of faith and hope in the future. We come to view our problems as overwhelming and feel we're not up to the task. But as we've seen, it doesn't have to be this way. Maintaining a sense of perspective on life's problems can be quite helpful, as can developing the ability to envision alternatives that aren't immediately evident. Taking thoughtful action to resolve problems, maintaining close and supportive relationships with others, and leading a balanced life that's characterized by a sense of accomplishment, enjoyment, faith, purpose, and personal effectiveness will also allow you to approach life's challenges with hope and confidence. While these approaches won't prevent loss, stress, adversity, or heartbreak—what Shakespeare referred to as "the slings and arrows of outrageous fortune"—they can alleviate the anxiety and worry that accompany them. Quite simply, they allow you to keep calm and carry on.

RESOURCES FOR READERS

Many excellent resources are available for people who are experiencing more significant forms of worry, anxiety, and fear. These include:

Academy of Cognitive Therapy (ACT), www.academyofct.org

American Board of Professional Psychology (cognitive and behavioral psychology board), www.abpp.org

Anxiety Disorders Association of America (ADAA), www.adaa.org

Association for Behavioral and Cognitive Therapies (ABCT), www.abct.org

International OCD Foundation, www.ocfoundation.org

Additional resources may be found on our website:
www.keepcalmthebook.com

REFERENCES

Abramowitz, J. S., D. F. Tolin, and G. P. Street. 2001. Paradoxical effects of thought suppression: A meta-analysis of controlled studies. *Clinical Psychology Review* 21 (5):683–703.

Adler, A. 1956. *The Individual Psychology of Alfred Adler: A Systematic Presentation in Selections of His Writings*, ed. H. L. Ansbacher and R. R. Ansbacher. New York: Basic Books.

Angelou, M. 1993. *Wouldn't Take Nothing for My Journey Now*. New York: Random House.

Antony, M. M., C. L. Purdon, V. Huta, and R. P. Swinson. 1998. Dimensions of perfectionism across the anxiety disorders. *Behaviour Research and Therapy* 36 (12):1143–54.

Beck, A. T. 1976. *Cognitive Therapy and the Emotional Disorders*. New York: International Universities Press.

Beck, A. T., G. Emery, and R. L. Greenberg. 1985. *Anxiety Disorders and Phobias: A Cognitive Perspective*. New York: Basic Books.

Borkovec, T. D., H. Hazlett-Stevens, and M. L. Diaz. 1999. The role of positive beliefs about worry in generalized anxiety disorder and its treatment. *Clinical Psychology and Psychotherapy* 6 (2):126–38.

Calamari, J. E., and A. S. Janeck. 1998. Intrusive thought in obsessive-compulsive disorder: Appraisal differences. *Depression and Anxiety* 7 (3):139–40.

Clark, D. M. 1986. A cognitive approach to panic. *Behaviour Research and Therapy* 24 (4):461–70.

Clark, D. M., and A. Wells. 1995. A cognitive model of social phobia. In *Social Phobia: Diagnosis, Assessment, and Treatment*, ed. R. G. Heimberg, M. R. Liebowitz, D. A. Hope, and F. R. Schneier, 69–93. New York: The Guilford Press.

Cosmides, L., and J. Tooby. 2000. Evolutionary psychology and the emotions. In *Handbook of Emotions*, 2nd ed., ed. M. Lewis and J. M. Haviland-Jones, 91–115. New York: The Guilford Press.

Csikszentmihalyi, M. 1990. *Flow: The Psychology of Optimal Experience*. New York: Harper and Row.

Davey, G. C. L., and A. Wells, eds. 2006. *Worry and Its Psychological Disorders: Theory, Assessment, and Treatment*. Chichester, UK: John Wiley and Sons.

Dugas, M. J., P. Gosselin, and R. Ladouceur. 2001. Intolerance of uncertainty and worry: Investigating specificity in a nonclinical sample. *Cognitive Therapy and Research* 25 (5):551–58.

Freddie Mac. 2008. Foreclosure avoidance research II: A follow-up to the 2005 benchmark study. freddiemac.com/service/msp/pdf/foreclosure_avoidance_dec2007.pdf (accessed January 18, 2010).

Freeman, A., and R. DeWolf. 1990. *Woulda, Coulda, Shoulda: Overcoming Regrets, Mistakes, and Missed Opportunities*. New York: HarperCollins.

Freeman, A., J. Pretzer, B. Fleming, and K. M. Simon. 1990. *Clinical Applications of Cognitive Therapy.* New York: Plenum Press.

Frijda, N. H. 1986. *The Emotions: Studies in Emotion and Social Interaction.* Cambridge, UK: Cambridge University Press.

Hope, D. A., R. G. Heimberg, H. A. Juster, and C. L. Turk. 2000. *Managing Social Anxiety: A Cognitive-Behavioral Therapy Approach—Client Workbook.* New York: Oxford University Press.

Marcks, B. A., and D. W. Woods. 2005. A comparison of thought suppression to an acceptance-based technique in the management of personal intrusive thoughts: A controlled evaluation. *Behaviour Research and Therapy* 43 (4):433–45.

Matthews, A., and C. MacLeod. 1994. Cognitive approaches to emotion and emotional disorders. *Annual Review of Psychology* 45:25–50.

Meeks, T. W., and D. V. Jeste. 2009. Neurobiology of wisdom: A literature review. *Archives of General Psychiatry* 66 (4):355–65.

Orsillo, S. M., and L. Roemer, eds. 2005. *Acceptance- and Mindfulness-Based Approaches to Anxiety: Conceptualization and Treatment.* New York: Springer Science and Business Media.

Power, M., and C. R. Brewin, eds. 1997. *The Transformation of Meaning in Psychological Therapies: Integrating Theory and Practice.* Chichester, UK: John Wiley and Sons.

Rachman, S. 1993. Obsessions, responsibility, and guilt. *Behaviour Research and Therapy* 31 (2):149–54.

Rachman, S., and P. de Silva. 1978. Abnormal and normal obsessions. *Behaviour Research and Therapy* 16 (4):233–48.

Reiss, S., and R. McNally. 1985. Expectancy model of fear. In *Theoretical Issues in Behavior Therapy*, ed. S. Reiss and R. R. Bootzin, 107–21. San Diego, CA: Academic Press.

Salkovskis, P. M. 1996. Cognitive-behavioral approaches to the understanding of obsessional problems. In *Current Controversies in the Anxiety Disorders*, ed. R. M. Rapee, 103–33. New York: The Guilford Press.

Sanderson, W. C., R. M. Rapee, and D. H. Barlow. 1989. The influence of an illusion of control on panic attacks induced via inhalation of 5.5% carbon dioxide–enriched air. *Archives of General Psychiatry* 46 (2):157–62.

Sternberg, R., and J. Jordan, eds. 2005. *A Handbook of Wisdom: Psychological Perspectives*. New York: Cambridge University Press.

Taylor, S., ed. 1999. *Anxiety Sensitivity: Theory, Research, and Treatment of the Fear of Anxiety*. Mahwah, NJ: Lawrence Erlbaum Associates.

Wells, A. 1995. Meta-cognition and worry: A cognitive model of generalised anxiety disorder. *Behavioural and Cognitive Psychotherapy* 23:301–20.

Wolpe, J. 1982. *The Practice of Behavior Therapy*. 3rd ed. New York: Pergamon Press.

Wright, J. H., M. Basco, and M. E. Thase. 2006. *Learning Cognitive-Behavior Therapy: An Illustrated Guide*. Arlington, VA: American Psychiatric Publishing.

Mark A. Reinecke, Ph.D., is professor of psychiatry and behavioral sciences and chief of the division of psychology at Northwestern University's Feinberg School of Medicine. He is a distinguished fellow and past president of the Academy of Cognitive Therapy, a diplomat of the American Board of Professional Psychology, and a fellow of the American Psychological Association and the Association for Psychological Science. He lives in Chicago, IL.

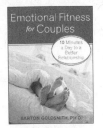

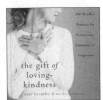